Our Land Was a Forest

TRANSITIONS: ASIA AND ASIAN AMERICA
Series Editor, *Mark Selden*

Our Land Was a Forest: An Ainu Memoir, Kayano Shigeru

The Political Economy of China's Financial Reforms: Finance in Late Development, Paul Bowles and Gordon White

Reinventing Vietnamese Socialism: Doi Moi in Comparative Perspective, edited by William S. Turley and Mark Selden

FORTHCOMING

Privatizing Malaysia: Rents, Rhetoric, Realities, edited by Jomo Kwame Sundaram

The Politics of Democratization: Vicissitudes and Universals in the East Asian Experience, edited by Edward Friedman

City States in the Global Economy: Industrial Restructuring in Hong Kong and Singapore, Tai-lok Lui, Stephen Chiu, and Kong-chong Ho

The Origins of the Great Leap Forward, Jean-Luc Domenach

Japanese Labor and Labor Movements, Kumazawa Makoto

Unofficial Histories: Chinese Reportage from the Era of Reform, edited by Thomas Moran

The Middle Peasant and Social Change: The Communist Movement in the Taihang Base Area, 1937–1945, David Goodman

Twentieth-Century China: An Interpretive History, Peter Zarrow

Moving Mountains: Women and Feminism in Contemporary Japan, Kanai Yoshiko

Workers in the Cultural Revolution, Elizabeth Perry and Xun Li

The Chinese Triangle and the Future of the Asia-Pacific Region, Alvin So and Hsin-Huang Michael Hsiao

Our Land Was a Forest

An Ainu Memoir

Kayano Shigeru

with a Foreword by
MIKISO HANE

translated by
Kyoko Selden and Lili Selden

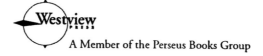

Westview
PRESS
A Member of the Perseus Books Group

Westview Press is grateful to the Japan Foundation for its financial assistance in publication of this volume.

Transitions: Asia and Asian America

Photo on the paperback cover and title page is of the autumn forest in Hokkaidō, Japan. Courtesy of Glenn Asakawa. The designs appearing with chapter and section headings are based on patterns from Ainu robes designed in the Nibutani area of Hokkaidō.

Published in 1994 in the United States of America by Westview Press, Inc., 5500 Central Avenue, Boulder, Colorado 80301-2877, and in the United Kingdom by Westview Press, 36 Lonsdale Road, Summertown, Oxford OX2 7EW

Originally published in Japanese under the title *Ainu no ishibumi.*
This translation published by arrangement with Mr. Shigeru Kayano.

Library of Congress Cataloging-in-Publication Data
Kayano, Shigeru.
  [Ainu no ishibumi. English]
  Our land was a forest : an Ainu memoir / Kayano Shigeru ;
translated by Kyoko Selden and Lili Selden.
    p.   cm. –– (Transitions—Asia and Asian America)
  List of the author's works: p. 172.
  ISBN 0-8133-1707-X. — ISBN 0-8133-1880-7 (pbk.)
  1. Ainu.   I. Title.   II. Series.
DS832.K36913   1994
952.4—dc20   93-45707
                                                                          CIP

Published by Westview Press, A Member of the Perseus Books Group

Printed and bound in the United States of America

Contents

Illustrations

Foreword

THIS IS AN ABSORBING ACCOUNT of Ainu life written by an Ainu striving to preserve his people's cultural heritage and sense of nationhood. Unlike many accounts by outsiders, which impose predetermined socio-anthropological categories on indigenous cultures, Kayano Shigeru offers a living testimonial to the history, ethos, customs, beliefs, hopes, and aspirations of a people whose way of life has been undermined by successive waves of invasion of their homeland by the Japanese.

The author's candid account of the history of three generations of his family, and through them of a people, draws us into the world of the Ainu, enhancing our understanding of and empathy for a way of life that prizes the harmony of human society in nature. It vividly reveals the tribulations that the Ainu endured as the Japanese occupied their home (*mosir*, the quiet land) and barred them from the subsistence hunting and fishing that provided the foundations of society and culture.

The process of encroachment began hundreds of years ago with incursions by Japanese warlords. The loss of land and livelihood accelerated with the establishment of the Meiji state, which brought the Ainu homeland under ever more stringent control and sought to "Japanize" the Ainu while incorporating Hokkaidō within the purview of an expansive empire.

Our Land Was a Forest recounts the story of a remarkable Ainu leader raised in an impoverished but culturally rich family, who ended his formal education after graduating from elementary school and as a youth earned his living as a forester. Eventually, drawing on cultural traditions he absorbed from the ballads his grandmother sang and the ancient legends she recounted, he dedicated his life to preserving Ainu heritage, values, language, arts, crafts, and customs—including dance, song, folklore, and literature—and to restoring the land and rights of his people. As a writer, as founder-curator of an important Ainu museum, and as a political activist, he has played a central role in the rebirth of Ainu consciousness. Kayano Shigeru's story is an invaluable record of a people and culture at the edge of extinction striving to preserve their integrity and their culture.

Mikiso Hane
Knox College

Translators' Note

THIS PROJECT WAS UNDERTAKEN at the suggestion of Matsuzawa Hiroaki, then of Hokkaidō University and presently of the International Christian University. Jane Marie Law of Cornell University read the entire manuscript with painstaking care and greatly improved the translation. Sasha Vovin of the University of Michigan assisted with romanization of the long quotations in Chapter 12. Kozaki Shinji checked the Ainu-language portions throughout the book and kindly provided romanization of all Ainu language portions of the text as well as syllable by syllable explanation. Sakurai Shin drew the two maps of Hokkaidō and the illustrations of the family insignia of the author's ancestors who settled in Hidaka county. In the fall of 1992 and 1993, students in the third-year Japanese reading course at Cornell read excerpts from Chapter 6 in the original and added to the spirit of the translation. Alice Colwell and Michelle Asakawa of Westview Press refined the language and format of the book. The author, Kayano Shigeru, extended warm support from Nibutani and provided a new epilogue and photographs, including a treasured original portrait of his grandparents. Suzusawa Shoten, Tokyo, kindly granted us the use of eight drawings from their *Ainu no mingu* (1978).

In the text and Glossary, Japanese names are given in the Japanese style, with family names first. In Matsuura Takeshirō, for example, Matsuura is the family name, Takeshirō the personal name. The Ainu portions of the text were translated from the Japanese translations provided by Kayano Shigeru in the original version of the book; hence the translation may sometimes lack line-to-line correspondence with the Ainu. Minimal punctuation was added to prose sections of the originally unpunctuated Ainu text.

Kyoko and Lili Selden

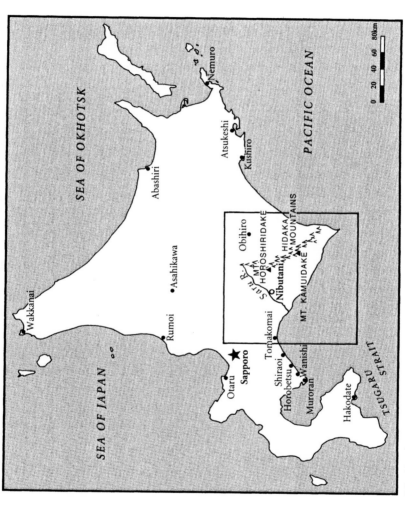

The island of Hokkaidō

Our Land Was a Forest

Our Nibutani Valley

THE AZURE HORIZON spreads in all directions, not a cloud in sight. The pine grove on the opposite shore of the Saru River is dark, but everything else in the vast landscape is pure white, covered with snow. The first time southerners see this Hokkaidō winter scene, they are likely to feel it would somehow be wrong to step into it. I myself felt such reluctance when I first went south and faced the grass that everywhere made the earth green.

Surveying the strikingly clear sky and the distant, dark pine grove across the river, I made my way over the bright snow to pay a visit to the ailing Kaizawa Turusino.

Standing in front of the old woman's house, I noticed a *hureayusni* decorating the upper right corner of the entrance. *Hureayusni*, or a branch of raspberry, was used as a charm to ward off colds. When I was a child, if word spread that a cold was making the rounds of a nearby village, every Ainu family put up raspberry branches either at the entrance of their reed-thatched home or by a window.

Turusino's house, like all Ainu homes these days, was a modern cement-block building that resists the cold. Yet this woman in her nineties was unhesitatingly carrying out this long-forgotten custom. The sight of that single branch carried me back forty years to my childhood.

In the early 1930s our Nibutani home was in the distinctive Ainu style, with a wood frame and a roof of thatched reed layers. The boards that served as walls, nailed on from the outside, were just 1 centimeter thick, and they were so warped that a hand could easily fit between the slats. So as winter approached, my mother and older sister prepared large amounts of glue with which to paste sheets of newspaper inside, hoping somehow to keep the snow and wind from blowing in.

I have a photograph of Nibutani in winter taken quite a bit later, in 1939, by the Italian ethnologist Fosco Maraini. As it shows, my home was just a single building without any food storage hut or tool shack; all that stood next to the house was an outhouse. It was the chilly dwelling of the poor.

But outside of it we children played to our heart's content, racing around in the snow and sledding. Although we wore long un-

In Ainu a house is called ciset, *from* ci *(we) and* set *(floor to sleep on). The roofs and walls of the houses shown here, restored for the Nibutani Museum of Ainu Cultural Resources, are made of thatch, which keeps the rooms unexpectedly warm.*

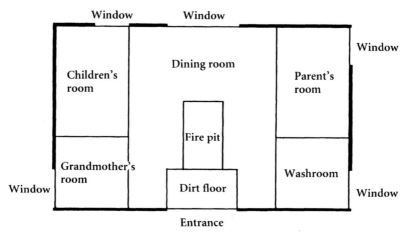

The plan of the Kaizawa house

derwear, split at the thighs, all we had on top were extra layers over our summer kimonos. If in my excitement I slid down too steep a hill, my kimono would flap open. The snow would come in through the slits of my long underwear, leaving me gasping for breath as it fell onto my penis. As I forgot myself in our games, my hands would stiffen up, and my penis, small enough to begin with, would shrink to the size of a kidney bean.

That was when I would finally miss home. Then I would run with all my might, warming my hands by putting them in my mouth or blowing on them. The moment the house came into sight, I would burst into tears. My mother, hearing me blubbering, would come out of the house and brush off the snow frozen onto my rear end or the hem of my kimono. She would then take my bright red, icy hands inside her robe and warm them between her breasts.

At that time my family consisted of nine members: my grandmother (born in 1850), my parents, an older sister, two elder brothers, myself, and two younger brothers. It was a rather hectic household, all of us crowding into a space of about 40 square meters.

We had a fire pit in the floor about 90 by 180 centimeters. In each of the two corners closest to the master's seat was a sunken-stump 10 centimeters in diameter. These stumps of catalpa, the bark still on, were my father's carving stands, and it was there that he made the many tools we needed in daily life. The tables wore down after several years of use, so Father would pull them out of the fire pit and take them to the altar outside the house. There he would lay them out with millet and cigarettes, offering prayers along the lines of "Please take these gifts back to the land of the gods." The new stumps were installed only after this ritual was performed.

A fire shelf hung above the fire pit. It was about the same size as the pit and had two functions. It ensured that sparks from the fire would not rise to the roof and set it aflame, and it served as a drying shelf for stalks of millet. The shelf was just the right height for a seven-year-old child to bump his head against, and around that age, when I stood up suddenly, I often did hit my head. My grandmother and parents would laugh, saying, "Good, good, it means you're growing. It's just as painful for the shelf. Comfort it by blowing on the spot where you bumped it." I would fight against the pain and, holding back my tears, blow earnestly on the shelf where I had run into it.

My grandmother, too, always sat in a fixed place. It was at the center of one edge of the fire pit, to the right of my father's seat. In front of her in the pit stood a *kanit,* a divided stick for winding thread. As Huci (Grandmother) wound the thread she had twisted with her fingertips onto the spindle, she would relate Ainu folktales, called *uwepekere,* to us grandchildren. Of course, she told them in Ainu.

I was her favorite, and Huci would start with "Shimeru" (she could not pronounce "Shigeru"). Once I answered, she would slowly start the tales, never once stopping her work at the spindle. There was a great variety of stories, interwoven with practical bits of wisdom for carrying out daily activities and lessons for life: One must not arbitrarily cut down trees, one must not pollute running water, even birds and beasts will remember kindnesses and return favors, and so on. One of the most often-repeated tales was about a child who was considerate of the elderly, praised by other people and the gods, and grew up to become a happy and respected adult.

In addition to the *uwepekere*, Huci also told us many, many *kamuy yukar*, or tales in verse about the Ainu gods. A god dwells in each element of the great earth mentioned in these tales, she would tell us, in the mountains off in the distance from Nibutani, the running waters, the trees, the grasses and flowers. Those gods looked just like humans, spoke the same language, slept at night, and worked by day in the land of the gods. As a child, I trustingly accepted as truth these tales about the gods.

Huci died in 1945 at the age of ninety-five. She had been a superb personal tutor when I was growing up, and it is thanks to her that I speak fluent Ainu and came to take pride in my ancestry. One day, when I was four or five years old, we were walking to the home of relatives about 2 kilometers away. As we approached the Kenasipaomanay, a little creek below the Nibutani communal graveyard, Huci called out, "*Kukor son ponno entere*" (Grandson, wait a moment for me).

As I stood still, she put aside her cane, sat down at the edge of the creek, and removed her black cloth headdress. Washing her hands and face in the creek, she turned to me and said, "Wash yourself off, too, Shimeru." When I did as she told me, she impressed upon me, young as I was, "You're going to grow up, and your *huci* will die. Whenever you pass this creek after I'm gone, I want you to remember that this is where you washed with your *huci*."

Nowadays, the roads around Kenasipaomanay are completely paved, and not a trace of the landscape back then remains. Even fifty years later, however, I always recall my grandmother when I pass by that area. I can thus say that her wish to live on in her grandson's heart, even after she was gone, has been fulfilled.

6

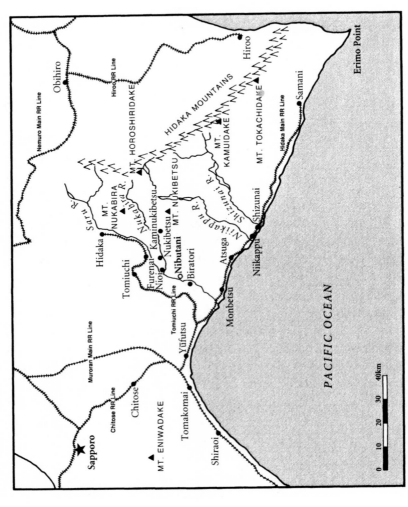

Detail of south-central Hokkaidō

This Nibutani, where I was raised in material poverty yet with spiritual wealth, is in the town of Biratori, located in the Saru region of Hidaka county, Hokkaidō.[1] From Tomikawa Station on the Hidaka main line, which runs along the southern shoreline from Tomakomai to Erimo on the national railway, it is about 20 kilometers inland by National Highway 237. This is the warmest region of Hokkaidō, with the least snowfall. The Saru River flows near here, and rice paddies abound. In the past, salmon were plentiful in the river, and in the nearby mountains there were deer and hare.

The Ainu had settled long ago in the Saru River region, with its mild climate and rich supply of food, dotting the landscape with their communities. I believe it is to the Saru that Ainu culture can trace its origins, for the *kamuy yukar* state that the river is the land of Okikurmikamuy. This is the god who taught folk wisdom to the Ainu: how to build houses, fish, raise millet, and so forth.

We Saru River Ainu prided ourselves on being from the land where the god Okikurmikamuy was born. Whenever we greeted Ainu from neighboring hamlets, we first identified ourselves in the following manner: "I am So-and-so, living and working in the village to which Okikurmikamuy descended from the heavens and taught us our folk wisdom." The other person would take a step back and welcome us respectfully, replying, "Ah, you're So-and-so of the village where the god Okikurmikamuy lived."

It was not until recently that I discovered the origins of the name *Nibutani*, which lies at about the midpoint of the Saru River. An acquaintance by the name of Nagai Hiroshi brought me an 1892 map on which the valley and its surroundings were labeled *Niputay*, which must come from *nitay*. *Nitay* means woods, forest,

---

1. Hokkaidō is divided into fourteen counties.

jungle. It was this map that finally made me realize the evolution of the Japanized name, Nibutani.

I have also encountered other proof to support my belief that Nibutani was a richly wooded area. About 6 kilometers from Nibutani, in the township proper of Biratori, there is a buckwheat noodle shop called the Fujiwara Eatery. Fujiwara Kan'ichirō, from the generation preceding the shop owners, first came to Biratori as a lumber dealer. He used to tell me, "I've logged all over, but the katsura in Nibutani were the best in Hokkaidō. It wasn't unusual to find trees 2 meters thick. They were so fine I once had a sawyer cut out a section for me to make a table." Even now, that impressive surface, made from a single piece of wood 150 centimeters wide, graces a table in the Fujiwara Eatery.

With just a glance at that piece of katsura, I—a woodcutter for twenty years—can still conjure up images of the dense woods in the mountains behind Nibutani: It was a forest of katsura, with herds of deer roaming through it. Whenever the Ainu needed meat, they entered the woods with bows and arrows and hunted as many deer as they desired. Sometimes they made *sakankekam*, or dried venison, and stored it. And in the Saru River, whose pure water flows beneath the mountain with its beautiful katsura woods, salmon struggled upstream in the autumn. The Ainu caught only as many salmon as they needed and, removing the innards, split the fish open to dry or smoked them for later use. Long before my time, Nibutani was such a fertile region.

During the Edo period, however, the *shamo* (mainland Japanese)[2] came into the area and, finding the Ainu living in this vast and rich landscape, forced them to labor as fishermen. Then in the Meiji era the *shamo* started taking over on a larger scale. (I expand on the history of the oppression of the Ainu in later chap-

---

2. *Shamo* is from a Japanized pronunciation of the Ainu word *sam* (side, neighbor).

ters.) Ignoring the ways of the Ainu, who had formulated hunting and woodcutting practices in accordance with the cycles of nature, the *shamo* came up with arbitrary "laws" that led to the destruction of the beautiful woods of Nibutani for the profit of "the nation of Japan" and the corporate giants. With this, half of the Nibutani region ceased to be a land of natural bounty.

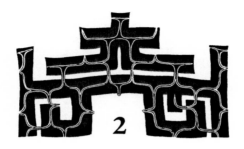

2

The Four Seasons in the Ainu Community

I GO BACK NOW to the early 1930s, to the earliest of my memories. We Ainu children in Nibutani played a number of games: Let me start with springtime. The first greens to shoot up in the spring are *makayo* (butterburrs). Next come *kunawnonno* (multipetaled buttercups), hardy plants that blossom even when the earth is still frozen solid. The flowers are not fragrant, but they are a magnificent golden hue. The Ainu valued this color highly, as reflected in a phrase reserved for the praise of superior treasures: "A jeweled sword of the gods, as fine as if it were uprooted from a dewdrop on the blossom of a *kunawnonno*." We children plucked these flowers, so cherished by adults, by the handful, and amused ourselves by decorating tree branches with them.

Until about the middle of April, frost and sheets of ice still formed. Taking advantage of the cold, we made "ice candy." We would cut diagonal incisions in a sugar maple, as one does with rubber trees, and use a withered stem of giant knotweed as a cylinder to catch the milky white, sweet syrup—*nitope*—that dripped out. Later we broke open the cylinder, removed the ice candy inside, and licked it. The word *nitope* comes from *ni*, which means tree in Ainu, and *tope*, or milk. The sugar maple, called *topeni* in

A kotan *was an Ainu hamlet of four or more houses surrounding a spring. It was constructed on high ground to be safe from floods and tidal waves. This residence is part of a model* kotan *recreating a village from early Taishō (1912–1926).*

Ainu, is the only maple with sweet syrup. Boiling 5.4 liters of syrup resulted in about a quarter liter of candy. Sucking this candy was a favorite spring pastime.

Yet another fun activity for us hungry children was gathering *peneemo*, literally, squashed potatoes. We would go to the potato fields that had been dug up in the fall and collect all the potatoes that had been left behind. These potatoes, which had frozen during the winter underneath the snow, were thawed on the arrival of

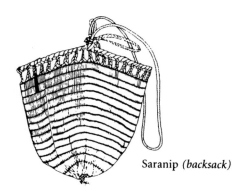

Saranip *(backsack)*

spring and thus had flattened by the time they were exposed to greet us. There were very few left in those carefully uprooted fields, and we were happy if we found twenty or thirty to put in our small *saranip* bags.[1]

We first washed off the potatoes with water and skinned them with our fingers. Next we pounded the *peneemo* in a mortar, then roasted and ate them. Or we peeled and dried them to save for a later occasion, when we added water before eating them. This was an ingenious method of preservation invented in an age when sustenance could not be treated lightly. Many of the newcomers from the mainland must have learned from the Ainu how to eat these potatoes. We also artificially created *peneemo* ourselves, leaving bruised or dwarf-sized potatoes to freeze in the fields or on our rooftop.

Around this time, too, we dug up *putaemo*, bulbs of a wild grass shaped like miniature potatoes. We children pulled them up if we got hungry while we were out playing, and chewed on them with gusto; *putaemo* are among the tastiest of foods that are edible raw.

We also peeled the outer skin of *putaemo* stalks and, cutting the white, pencil-like inside into 3-centimeter-long pieces, moistened

1. A *saranip* bag is woven from the bark tissue of the *shinanoki* tree and usually worn on one's back.

them in our mouths. When they were soft with our saliva, we manipulated them so they would make the sound *spon, spon.* Children called these stalks *spopon.*

By May the butterburrs grew to 15 or 20 centimeters in diameter. We pulled them up by the handful, peeled the skin from the root upward in one motion, and busily bit into them. Despite a slight bitterness, they were soft and tasty. When we ate them, our mouths turned black from the tangy juice, but no one minded since it did the same to all of us who ate.

Around this time, plowing started in the fields on the right bank of the Saru River. We walked behind the plow, picking up cutworms. Using these worms as bait, we set up a rope to catch quantities of a variety of red-bellied dace, a small, active clearwater fish. The rope had fishing line tied on at 30-centimeter intervals, and each line had a fishhook tied onto it for worms. My older brothers set up the traps, then sent me to check on them. The dace we caught were chopped into tiny pieces, bones and all, and thrown into soup. The dace season was from the middle of April through the end of May.

In June the first baby sparrows hatched. When it was almost time for the sparrows to leave the nest, we climbed up to the thatched rooftop, thrust our hands into the nest in the thatch, and removed a tiny sparrow from its warm shelter. Dangling the bird by the fuzzy tufts of its head, we would intone in Ainu, "*Ekotanu tapkar kiki, sapo tapkar kiki*" (Dance the dance of your village! Dance the dance of your sister!). Distressed at having its "hair" pinched, the sparrow would desperately beat its wings, turning its body around and around, as the parents chirped furiously and flew around the tormenters of their baby. When our parents discovered our antics, it became *our* turn to be suspended by the hair of our heads and to kick our legs in the air.

Ainu children, however, returned the sparrows to their nests without killing them. In the event a bird died from our over-enthusiasm, we would have a funeral, where we made offerings of millet and prayed, "Please take this gift back with you to the land of the gods."

In the mid-1920s the games of Ainu children were not so different from those of the *shamo*. We played at something called hoops for which we needed the wheel of an old horse-drawn wagon or bicycle. Since such wheels were hard to come by, they were very precious—especially bike wheels (in Nibutani in those days, only Nitani Kunimatsu, Kaizawa Matsuo, Kaizawa Zensuke, and the Matsuzaki shop owned bikes). We usually settled for bamboo hoops tied around barrels. Playing with hoops involved bending the tip of a rather thick wire in the shape of a question mark, placing it on the curve of the hoop, and walking or running while pushing the hoop with the wire to make the hoop roll.

We also played on wooden stilts that were essentially the same as those called "bamboo horse" elsewhere in Japan, but modified since thick bamboo does not grow in Hokkaidō. We called the stilts "tall horse," which I thought simply meant that one got tall when walking on them.[2] To make these stilts we went to a nearby mountain and cut stalks of the right thickness.

Girls bounced rubber balls to a song that went:

> **Negotiations collapsing,**
> **the Russo-Japanese war began.**
> **Russian soldiers quickly fled;**
> **Japanese soldiers feared no death.**
> **He led a force of 50,000**
> **and killed all but six.**
> **At the battle of July 8th,**
> **he went all the way to Harbin**

---

2. In Japanese "tall horse" is *takauma* and "bamboo horse" *takeuma*. Because of the proximity of sounds, *takauma* nicely substituted for *takeuma*. As a child, the author did not recognize the original association of *taka* (tall) and *take* (bamboo).

and struck down Kropotkin.
Long live General Tōgō!

This song was then popular among children throughout Japan. Another ball-bouncing song was a counting song made up mostly of place names that started with the same syllable as the numbers one to ten in Japanese: "One sen,[3] two Niigata, three Mikawa, four Shinshū, five Kōbe, six Musashi, seven Nagoya, eight Hakodate, nine Kyūshū, ten Tokyo, Kyōto, Ōsaka, Momoyama, Nara, sightseeing, three, then four."

We also played split bamboo. Because we had no bamboo, we cut up a flagpole or the handle of an old broom into 25-centimeter lengths, split each into widths of about 2 centimeters, and shaved them neatly so that the splinters wouldn't hurt our hands. Four sticks made a set that each of us held tightly then threw into the air, trying to keep the pieces as close together as possible and to catch them over and over again as they fell. There was a counting song for this game, too: "First throw, second throw, miso-seller's bride, when did she come …"—I've forgotten the rest, but it was with such simple games that we passed the time. Jumping rope and stone skipping were popular as well.

Of course these games were not unique to Ainu children. Others, though, may have been indigenous Ainu games. One of these was making toy *pattari* in the creek when the snow thawed in spring. *Pattari* can be likened to the Japanese "deer repeller," a scarecrow-like device that used water. *Pattari* were made from hollow stalks of garden sorrel filled with creek water. With the accumulation of water, one end of the stalk dropped onto the earth under the weight. On the rebound, the other end hit the ground with a thump. In those days, there were over ten real *pattari* in the

---

3. There are 100 sen to 1 yen.

Pon-osat creek to the east of Nibutani Primary School. Adults used them to pound grains such as millet.

Then there was *seypirakka* (shell clogs). A hole was bored through the shell of a large surf clam and a thick rope passed through it. We wore two clams each, with the rope between our first two toes, and walked or ran about on them. The shells made a clicking noise like horseshoes, so we pretended to be horses. To make the holes in the seashells, we burned the tip of a young bush clover branch; when it turned red, we touched it to the seashell and blew on it. After many repetitions, the spot on the shell became white and brittle, and we could open a hole with the light tap of a nail. We children were copying the method adults used to make *pipa*, seashell knives for cutting the ears of millet.

When spring passed and summer came, our happiest pastime was canoeing in the Saru River. An old ferryman by the name of Kaizawa Kinjirō would lend us his canoe free if we were with an older child, so that we could practice boating. He was generous with the canoe when the water was low but never let us borrow it when the water level had suddenly risen during a long rainy spell or after a torrential rain. Since a schoolboy named Kaizawa Nobuo had drowned in a mishap, the ferryman had become even more cautious.

But we were always so keen on getting into the canoe that we would furtively push it into the current and jump in. When we got to just the right depth, the older boys would grab those children who could not swim and throw them into the water. The children would thrash their limbs about as they gulped air until the current carried them back to the shallows. However crude this kind of swimming lesson seems, children learned much faster than if they were taught step by step. This was how Ainu children used to master canoeing and swimming.

In summer the villagers fished for trout in the Saru River. Trout that yearly migrate back from the sea stay in the deep waters of the river's main current until the time comes to move on to smaller streams. In order to catch them there, adults brought nets to a depth where the water reached above their heads, and while someone held one end of a net at the shallows, another swam toward the deep with the other end. The two then chased the trout into the net by rolling the net inward.

It was fun catching not only large fish like trout but *cep posunankar,* or small clearwater fish. First we made arrows called *peraai.* A relatively fat stalk of ordinary rush was used for the shaft of the arrow, and a 4- or 5-centimeter-wide wooden tablet was attached at the tip. Once night came, we took these *peraai* to a small stream, lit torches made of birch bark, and with them as our guides, slowly waded from the lower to the upper reaches of the stream. The slow movements of the dace, sculpin, and loach, disturbed in their sleep, were illuminated in the torchlight. We then struck them—slap!—with the *peraai* and caught them. This method of fishing, called *sune* (light), was a delightful game on summer nights.

Summer in the *kotan* (hamlet) of Nibutani was short, and autumn always followed close behind. Then would begin the salmon fishing that called forth the best in the Ainu. I cannot begin to imagine how many salmon in the old days swam up the Saru River, then called the Sisirimuka. The *kamuy yukar* that my grandmother used to sing for me described the salmon as swelling the water surface like a seismic wave as they swam against the current, "the backs of those swimming near the surface being scorched by the sun, and the bellies of those swimming near the bottom of the water nearly scraped off by rocks." By 1932 or 1933, about the time of my earliest memories, such great numbers of salmon no longer came up river. Still, there were more than enough for us to eat every day. Of course we never fished to excess.

For salmon fishing we used nets and hooks. The net, made of a heavy-duty cotton thread, was approximately 1.3 by 2.7 meters. A 3-centimeter-wide, 2.1-meter-long stick was tied to each end of the net. Four men boarded two dugout canoes, and while one in each maneuvered the canoe, the other held one stick of the net. Rowing downstream so that the canoes formed an inverted V-shape, they let the net float in the water. When salmon entered the V, the men moved their canoes together and, wringing the net as they pulled it up, caught the fish in what was now like a hammock. This was one of several fishing methods and was called *yasi* (scooping).

My father, Kaizawa Seitarō (1893–1956), was very fond of salmon fishing—or perhaps he was simply desperate to catch salmon because his family could not survive without them. When he caught the first salmon of the year, he placed it on a cutting board at the master's seat to the side of the fireplace, with the salmon's head pointing toward the fire and its belly toward the left of the fireplace. Sitting to the right of the fireplace, my father bowed ceremonially to the salmon and said in Ainu, "Thank you for honoring us with your presence at our house today." Then he faced the flames in the fireplace and prayed to the goddess of fire: "Today, for the first time this year, I have brought home a salmon. Please rejoice. This salmon is not merely for us humans to eat by ourselves, but for us to eat with the gods and with my children, as tiny as insects. Please watch over me, that I may catch many salmon hereafter."

When the prayer was over, the salmon was cut up and stewed in a big pot. As the chunks were put into the pot, my brother and I were sent out to invite the neighborhood grandmothers. Sometimes, we were sent off in the dark at one or two o'clock in the morning. "Grandma, Dad's stewing the autumn salmon he caught, so come along right away to eat with us." When my brothers and I arrived back home after circling through the neighborhood shouting this message, those who had responded quickly were already seated at the fireside. Often, by the time the neighbors and we finished eating the salmon as all of us surrounded the fire, the eastern sky was dawning white. When the grandmothers left to go home, my father let each take a salmon if there had been a big catch; if not, he gave each just enough for one skewer, saying in Ainu, "Please share this with all the gods through the goddess of fire in your house." Nor was his sharing limited to the first salmon of the year; my father often treated the old women who could not go fishing themselves. (This may sound as if there were only old women in our neighborhood, and in fact there were quite a few of them.)

Although we were poor, the whole house bustled with cheerfulness during the salmon season. When there was a big catch, we could exchange the salmon for rice, and we spent many a day thereafter enjoying our relative prosperity. Even salmon roe, which was out of our reach during the rest of the year, appeared on the dinner table as a side dish to go with our rice. We also ate a rice porridge called *ciporosayo*, prepared by adding heaping servings of salmon roe to rice boiled with millet. We savored the light red roe in the salty porridge, picking up one egg at a time with our chopsticks. A close look revealed a deeper red tinge in the center of each egg. I used to wonder in my child's mind why the whole thing did not turn such a red.

We also prepared limited quantities of a certain delicacy: salmon air bladders filled with salmon roe. The roe we used for this was *marotkeciporo*, the kind found right before the fish spawn. *Marotkeciporo*, unlike the connected eggs of early roe, separate easily. We salted them lightly, stuffed them into air bladders, then dried them on the rack over the fire pit. We enjoyed eating the dried eggs one at a time, as a snack. Thinking back, I must say they were luxurious snacks indeed. (Among the ancient *uwepekere*, there is a story about giving a stuffed salmon bladder to a fox disguised as an Ainu. Unlike a human being, who would eat one egg at a time, the fox put the whole air bladder into its mouth. The roe therefore stuck to its teeth, and the fox finally revealed its true form.)

Once the pleasant autumn had passed, around mid-November, sleet began to fall and then changed to snow. With each sleet storm, the days became colder; winter was unmistakably approaching. My mother would go out to an open field nearby to gather reeds, which she carried home to thatch the roof. She would then make a screen to protect the house against the wind and snow. Another big task before winter was to make a new toilet. Since outhouse toilets in the northern region freeze and rise, we had to dig a very deep hole for the new toilet. By the time that was ready, the real, north-country winter was on its way.

As I have already described the activities of Ainu children in winter, I will not repeat them here. Suffice it to say that my early years in elementary school were spent in the midst of bountiful nature and kind, though poor, people.

3

My Grandfather, a Slave to the Shamo

MY SURNAME IS KAYANO, but I was born the third son of Kaizawa Seitarō and Hatsume on June 15, 1923. My surname differs from that of my parents because as soon as I was born, I was adopted by the Kayanos, the family into which my father's older sister had married. For some reason, I was raised by my parents instead of being taken to the Kayano family.

Here I would like to mention my ancestry. According to my father, our forebears came from Tokachi, the great plain facing the Pacific. Crossing the Hidaka mountain range, which runs north and south, splitting the southern half of the main portion of Hokkaidō, they migrated to Hidaka, an area west of the range, and settled in Shizunai and Hae. Shizunai was the site of the Samkusaynu incident during the Edo period,[1] when the Ainu rose against the oppression of Matsumae, the Japanese province on the southwest tip of the forked peninsula, Ojima, that stretches toward the main island of Japan.

---

1. Samkusaynu led an Ainu rebellion against the Matsumae Japanese in 1669. Matsumae, the only Japanese province in Hokkaidō during the Edo period, was notorious for the exploitation of the Ainu that went on there.

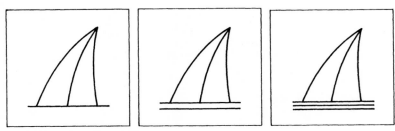

Aysirosi *of the author's forebearers*

Three brothers—it is unclear whether they were original settlers in Hidaka or their children—left Shizunai to set up separate
homes. As they parted from one another, the brothers talked
about designing a new *aysirosi* different from the one they had
used in Tokachi. The *aysirosi* is an inscription carved at the end of
a poisoned trap arrow used for hunting bear and deer; an insignia
is necessary because a bear or a deer shot with such an arrow did
not die instantly but wandered far off from the trap as the poison
gradually took effect. Once the bear was skinned and gutted, the
insignia on the arrow showed whose trap had felled the animal.
An insignia was therefore crucial.

After a consultation, the three brothers, who had lived as fishermen on the coast of Hidaka, agreed to model their new insignia
after *asipenoka,* the dorsal fin of not just any fish but of the killer
whale, sharp enough to kill another whale.

The three men determined that the dorsal-fin insignia of the
oldest brother should have a single horizontal line underneath;
the middle brother's, double horizontal lines; and the third
brother's, triple horizontal lines. They then swore that whenever
they came across one of these three inscriptions, they would help
one another in affirmation of their common ancestry.

The youngest brother, who had the third insignia, came to
Sisirimuka (the Saru River), and he is our direct ancestor—in
other words, the insignia of my family's trap arrows is the
asipenoka killer with three horizontal stripes underneath. One day
the young man with the *aysirosi* of three lines beneath a dorsal fin

retraced the Saru River to Pipaus Kotan (a traditional name for one part of Nibutani Village). The elders of the village thought this youth somehow confidence-inspiring and decided to give him a wife so he would settle in the village. This was not all that unusual a situation and was called *menoko epeka aweham,* "providing a wife to stop a man's feet."

True to the villagers' expectations, the young man turned out to be an excellent hunter and, moreover, an unparalleled orator. One day an insignificant matter led to a dispute between Pipaus Kotan and another village, and an *ukocaranke* was initiated. The word *uko* means "mutually," and *caranke* means "to let words fall"; the compound word *ukocaranke* thus refers to the Ainu custom of settling differences by arguing exhaustively. It also implies that the Ainu do not solve disputes by violence.

Caranke requires the talent to argue with logic and the physical strength to sit in debate for days. Probably in recognition of his double gift in oratory and physical strength, the man with the three-lined dorsal-fin insignia was chosen as the *caranke* representative of Pipaus Kotan.

Over a period of six days and nights, this man continued to argue without once collapsing, and he led the dispute to a peaceful solution. The villagers were overjoyed. Although his formal Ainu name is lost to us, the villagers from then on called him Awaankur (the Seated Man) in honor of his oratorical skills and physical endurance.

This is the extent of my knowledge of Awaankur, our ancestor five generations back. Awaankur had a son by the name of Inisetet (To Scoop Things). His name appears in the "Saru Journal" (1858),[2] a diary left by Matsuura Takeshirō, who explored the Saru

2. This unpublished journal, in the possession of Japan's Ministry of Education, was made available to the author through Yamada Hidezō. Matsuura Takeshirō (1818–1888) was a government official of the late Edo period who explored Hokkaidō and the Kuriles, a chain of islands stretching to the northeast of

River during the Ansei era (1854–1860): "The head family of eight: Inisetet (60), his wife Irapekar (51), son Awetok (24), wife Akusake (22), younger brothers Totkaram (12) and Ikorohasiw (10), his younger sister Ikatosin (7), and another younger brother Ranhareha (5). The son and his wife and young brother Totkaram were drafted for labor." This is an excerpt from the entry on Pipaus Kotan. The younger brother Totkaram, who is mentioned along with Inisetet's son and his wife, is my grandfather. (I later discuss how they were "drafted for labor.")

My grandfather's name, Totkaram, was created from the words *tot* (to grow), *ka* (this), and *ramu* (to think or wish), and it carries a prayer: "May he grow into a fine person." He was born on January 18, 1847, and died on December 20, 1919, before I was born, so I know nothing about him directly. But there is one episode my grandmother Tekatte told me about him, saying, "*Itek eoirapnena*" ("You must not forget this story"). It is related to the entry in Matsuura Takeshirō's diary quoted above.

My grandfather Totkaram was the second son of Inisetet, an eloquent and popular chieftain, and the gentle Irapekar. He grew up uneventfully in the midst of a fertile, natural environment with his older brother, two younger brothers, and sister. In those days, however, it could be a source of sadness to Ainu parents when their children matured, for the *shamo* who came to the seashore then forcibly engaged them as laborers.

In the Edo period, Hokkaidō was placed under the provincial *shamo* government of the Matsumae clan. Because the province produced no rice, retainers received land instead of rice as income. That land was called a "location," and the retainer-landowners commissioned merchants and others to manage their "locations."

Hokkaidō. The ages given in the journal reflect the traditional way of counting. "Totkaram (12)" means he was in his twelfth year counting from birth, making him age eleven (or ten before his eleventh birthday).

Whether the "locations" were fishing spots or produced other goods from the sea, commissioners drafted the Ainu as their labor force. Remuneration was minimal and is said to have been one-seventh to one-fifth of what was paid to *shamo*. In this work the Ainu were nothing but slaves.

The "location" where Nibutani Ainu were taken as slaves was Atsukeshi. Over 350 kilometers from Nibutani, it is closer to Nemuro than the midpoint between Kushiro and Nemuro. Even now, with roads built, the shortest distance between the two places is 293 kilometers. At that "location," then the focal point of eastern Hokkaidō, labor was supplied exclusively by the Ainu. Since the Ainu population in Atsukeshi had been reduced by work-related deaths, *shamo* employed Ainu from the Saru and Yūfutsu areas.

Village chief Inisetet's fears finally came to pass. One day, "*tu tam ukaeotte sapaha ta pasikur roski roski, pekor oka sisam utar ek hine, apoho utar tura rusuy*": "*Sisam* came, wearing two swords at their waists and appearing to have crows resting on their heads, to propose taking villagers and their sons" to Atsukeshi.[3] Some people had already been taken to Atsukeshi and never returned, having died of cruel treatment there. Through an Ainu interpreter, Inisetet therefore declined the unjust offer.

In response the Japanese samurai put their hands on the hilts of their swords, appearing ready to unsheath them at any moment, and threatened to kill all the villagers unless the chief handed some over. A tearful Inisetet accepted their terms and decided to send his oldest son, Awetok, and Awetok's wife. The samurai, still unsatisfied, demanded the young Totkaram as well. Inisetet appealed to the samurai to leave the boy, only eleven years old and small for his age, saying that he would only be in their way if they

---

3. *Sisam*, from *si* (one's) and *sam* (neighbor), means mainland Japanese (as does *shamo*). The "crows" refer to the samurai's topknots.

took him along. The Japanese rejected Inisetet's supplication, however, stating that even a child was capable of carrying one salmon on his back.

When it was decided that the three would go, the samurai announced they would leave that very day. They probably knew from frequent experience that if they delayed their departure a day or two, the Ainu would flee into the mountains. That is apparently why on "Ainu-hunting" trips the *shamo* showed up without warning, as if to assault villagers in their sleep.

According to Matsuura Takeshirō's "Saru Journal" (quoted above), there were a total of 116 villagers who made up twenty-six households in Niputani (an old name for present-day Nibutani), Pipaus, and Kankan in 1858. Of these, forty-three men and women had been drafted for forced labor. My grandfather, Totkaram, at the age of eleven, was the youngest of them.

I would like to quote from the "Saru Journal" a passage related to Nibutani. Although it is rather long, I think it illustrates well what draft labor was like then:

> Of the twenty-seven households in villages called Nibutani, Honnifutani, and Residential Nifutani, there were nine households where we stopped to take a rest.
>
> A family of seven, including matriarch Kasitekusi (age 47), her son Ukarikusi (18), his younger brothers Arikatte (13) and Totekewri (12), his younger sister Cipeku, (10), his older sister Harutosika (32), her daughter Hirasitean (7). Of them, the son and one of the younger brothers have been drafted for labor.
>
> Next door to them, another family of seven, including patriarch Hakeanriru (48), his wife Uteosanu (48), their son Urahenka (13), his younger brother Ekekusite, (9), his younger sister Simukusite (7), another younger brother Uwekasan (5), an adopted son Kahutokupa (10). The family head and his first son have been drafted.
>
> Next door, a family of four: matriarch Harutoki (67), her son Hasikku (38), his wife Sarawe (27), their son (3). The family head has been drafted.

Next door, a family of three: matriarch Tarawesi (74), adopted daughter Usamatte (39), adopted son Itaknoa (19). The adopted son Itaknoa has been drafted.

Next door, a family of five: patriarch Sirimawsi (64), his son Itowemanu (37), his wife Kanruswe (28), their son Asikuniha (4), his younger sister (3). The son Itowemanu has been drafted.

Next door, a family of two: the family head Towsiro (45), his wife Yawetohe (44). The family head has been drafted.

Next door, a family of seven: the family head Hosoro (45), his son Tosiroku (28) and his wife Siyutarero (25), his younger sisters Mokeante (25), Sinuton (24), Hawemeki (18), Hawebusikaru (10). The son, his wife, and three of his sisters have been drafted; only the mother [*sic*] and the youngest girl remain at home.

Next door, a family of five: the family head Renkahuayno (46) and his wife Katorenu (48), their son Mawecasinu (13). The family head has been drafted.

All who were taken left needles and thread with those remaining.[4]

Pipaus: consists of fifteen households.

The head family of eight: Inisetet (60), his wife Irapekar (51), son Awetok (24), wife Akusake (20), younger brothers Totkaram [author's note: my grandfather] (12) and Ikorohasiw (10), his younger sister Ikatosin (7), and another younger brother Ranhareha (5). The son and his wife and young brother Totkaram were drafted for labor.

Next door to them, a family of six: matriarch Mukkoran (52), daughter Asirikawsi (31), her son Etamakaw (5) and another son (2), Asirikawsi's younger brother Tonramuku (23) and his wife Uweasi (21). Tonramuku and his wife have been taken.

Next door, a family of four: the family head Ikurukasan (42) and

---

4. At a time when clothes were made at home, needles and thread were treasured items.

his wife Tanehare (27), their son Torekaayno (9), his younger sister Atano (8). The family head has been drafted.

Next door, a family of five: patriarch Esahaayno (59) and his wife Tekeayo (48), their son Katawku (29) and his wife Akare (27), Katawku's younger brother Rikihawri (18) and younger sister Ciruso (11). The son, his wife, and his younger brother have been drafted, leaving the old couple and the youngest child.

Next door, a family of three: the family head Imonniku (51), his wife Arerisanke (26), and their son (2). The family head has been drafted, leaving his wife and child.

Next door, a family of five: the family head Itomesan (55) and his wife Reanke (46), their son Roretaku (34) and his wife Tekare (26), their boy (4). The son has been drafted.

Next door, a family of nine: the family head Sankuranu (52), his wife Kowesamure (47), their daughter Uwekarahe (27), Uwekarahe's son (5), his younger brother (2), Uwekarahe's younger sister Siyutoran (19), younger brother Kariwawku (14), younger sister Hosiwsi (11) and younger sister (8). [Author's note: The youngest daughter's name is not written, but judging from her older brother's and sisters' names, I am certain that this was my grandmother Tekatte.] The second daughter Siyutoran and the son Kariwawku have been drafted.

Next door, a family of three: the family head Hechiranke (58) and his wife Itaman (52), their son Husawri (27). The son has been taken.

Next door, a family of four: matriarch Ciniwkatte (44), her son Iyukutean (15), his younger sister Uratokka, another sister (3). The son has gone out for forced labor. The mother alone supports the two children.

Next door, a family of three: the family head Sanrekka (50) and his wife Sahiranka (47), their son Iramukute (23)—a family of three. The son has been drafted.

Next door, a family of two: the family head Asirikanna (60) and his wife Howasi (54).

Next door, a family of three: the family head Ikusankuru the old man (57), his son Tasareki (22), his sister Wente (16). Both brother and sister have been drafted, leaving just the father at home.

Next door, a family of five: the family head Sahakato (58), his wife Siutra, their son Anrasare (23) and his wife Konuan (19), his younger brother Sikewri (15). The son and his wife and his younger brother have been drafted.

Next door, a family of three: patriarch Yaekantana (44), his younger brother Irekuhori (41), his younger sister Kekere (17). Both the younger brother and sister have been drafted.

Next door, a family of four: the family head Kanimonte (41), his wife Sarokute (25), their son Wenotok (7), his sister (4). The family head has been drafted.

The above survey is based on the statements of the village chief Inisetet, Sirimawsu, and the old woman Kasitekusi.

Kankan: consists of three households.

A family of five: the family head Siyutosimawri (55), his wife Siasita (46), their adopted son and daughter's husband Ikasiyuku (27), his wife Uworemare (27), their sons (5 and 3), younger brothers Sarakawri (20) and Inukawri (16). The adopted son and Uworemare's two younger brothers have been drafted.

Next door, a family of two: the family head Imawrari (48), his wife Yawenunke (47)—a family of four. Both husband and wife seem to have been drafted for the duration of the fishing season.

Next door, a family of four: the family head Irawsite (40) and his wife Utekiunke (37), their son Kanehakute (7), another son (5). It seems that the family head has been drafted.

I have quoted at length in the belief that these passages serve as a monument to, or a requiem for, the Ainu of Nibutani in those days. I hope also to make known that it was Matsuura Takeshirō who, angered by the cruelty of Matsumae province and the "location" contractors, made repeated proposals that eventually led to the abolition of forced labor.

Inisetet and his fellow villagers wept with grief as they prepared to part with their wives, husbands, and children who were bound for Atsukeshi. They nevertheless sent the travelers off with old worn-out deerskin clothes, one or two changes of clothes, and woven mats for sleeping on the road at night. Carrying these items on their backs, those forced to leave Nibutani headed for Atsukeshi on foot, walking over 350 kilometers in silence. Theirs was a journey made not out of need but under threat of swords. How painful and long the route must have been—even if they had walked 30 kilometers a day, the trip would have taken twelve or thirteen days.

When the Ainu finally arrived at their work site in Atsukeshi, there wasn't a building to house them. Told to stake out their own sleeping spaces, they had no choice but to prepare makeshift lodgings, mainly using the woven mats they had carried from home. Later, they cut thatch and bamboo grass to put up huts where at night they sheltered themselves from the rain and dew; by day they were forced to engage in hard labor.

From the day he arrived at Atsukeshi, eleven-year-old Totkaram longed desperately to go home to Nibutani. It would have been no simple matter, however, to retrace the course that had taken more than ten days to walk.

The Ainu were beaten awake when the morning stars still glimmered and were forced to work until they could no longer see the ground at night. Since Totkaram was too small to fish, the Japanese master at the accounting desk—in Ainu, we called the desk *ponkanpi* (small paper) or *porokanpi* (large paper)—made him help in the kitchen. Totkaram's main work was to gather firewood and pump water, but even this was heavy labor for the young boy, and he cried every day as he worked.

One day, while he was cutting up fish with a *tasiro* (a big knife used in the mountains), an idea occurred to him. Rather than suffer such hardships at work until autumn or, more likely, until the snow started, he would cut off a finger and be sent home. He resolved to follow through with his plan, but when he imagined the pain, he was unable to carry it out. Several days passed.

As the days stretched on, work conditions became even harsher. In his intense desire to go home and at the limits of his endurance, he decided one morning to go ahead with his plan and rose early. He took the *tasiro* in his right hand and rested his left forefinger on the cutting board, then raised the knife. But his hands trembled, and he could not cut off his finger. He gave up for that day.

The following morning, he tried not to think of anything and, closing his eyes before his hands started to shake, swung the knife down with determination. He had meant to cut just so, near the tip, but his aim went awry because his eyes were closed. The knife hit so close to the base joint that his tiny finger snapped into the air. Although he had readied himself for the pain, it was so bad that he burst into a wail. Even as he cried, his one thought was that with such a major injury, he could now go home.

Hearing his cries, the master rushed to him, but the man's words only made him cry louder still. "What's all the fuss about just one finger! Cover it with salt and you'll be all right in two or three days." Totkaram had been certain that he would be sent home, and now that his hopes were thwarted, the wound ached all the more.

I don't know if he did apply salt, but much to his disappointment, the wound healed more quickly than expected. Every day he gazed upon the stump of his forefinger and bemoaned his lot. One day another idea occurred to him. Mixed in among the innumerable fish caught daily were many poisonous blowfish. Secretly collecting some, he squeezed out their bile and coated his whole body with it. After he had done this several times, his skin turned grayish yellow, and he looked as if he had what is now known as jaundice. Seeing Totkaram in this condition, the master thought the boy had contracted a terrible disease and ordered him sent home. Totkaram wanted to leap with joy but showed no hint of emotion in front of the master.

Whether he came home by himself or was brought home by an adult, I don't know, but he was finally able to return to the Nibutani he had so longed for. Although it came about because he had painted himself with poisonous fish bile, he had also lost his left forefinger from its base. How his parents, Inisetet and Irapekar, must have both rejoiced and grieved.

In a photograph taken in 1911, my grandfather Totkaram's lack of a left forefinger is clearly visible. He lived to be more than seventy, but when I think of the difficulties he encountered for sixty years because of the missing finger, I realize the great loss incurred from his journey to Atsukeshi.

The woman who became Totkaram's wife, in other words my grandmother Tekatte, also appears in Matsuura Takeshirō's "Saru Journal" (as noted earlier). The name Tekatte comes from *tek* (hand) and *atte* (to increase), and means "a worker is added." She, too, was once taken to Atsukeshi for forced labor.[5] According to what she told me, the terror she experienced on the way to Atsukeshi was even greater than the pain of hard labor.

One night, en route to Atsukeshi, as they camped in the mountains, they heard a beast growl, "brrrr, brrrr." Neither my grandmother nor the other women nor the men and children had ever heard such a growl, so they could not tell what kind of animal it was. The dog they had brought along barked, and the footsteps of the monster chasing the dog echoed clearly, but the sound did not

5. Author's note: On August 22, 1972, when I visited Nabesawa Nebuki (Ainu form Nepki) for a recording session at Saruba in Biratori, she mentioned that she had gone to Atsukeshi with my grandmother Tekatte.

The author's grandfather (left, his left forefinger missing) and grandmother (right), with their daughter Umon and granddaughter Haruno, 1911.

belong to either a bear or a deer. Terrified by the growls coming from the dark, my grandmother lay trembling all night, not sleeping a wink and calling on the gods for help.

When a faint dawn broke and they fearfully approached the direction of the noise, they found a long-headed or, rather, long-faced animal that was like neither bear nor deer. It was a horse. The Saru River Ainu, who had never seen a horse, had spent a sleepless night in the open, afraid of a horse's snorting. Whenever my grandmother told me about this, she first earnestly described how frightful it was, but then toward the end of the story, she would laugh, saying that it was owing to a horse, no longer a rarity, that she had thought she would not survive until morning.

The forced labor was cruel. Matsuura Takeshirō's *Kinsei Ezo jinbutsushi* (A record of modern Ainu individuals)[6] describes how Ainu were given a single bowl of rice a day or leftover rice watered down in the form of porridge, so that they became ill at age thirty or so, and their children died from hunger and cold. As already mentioned, the pay was, to use a common Japanese expression, "as little as a sparrow's tear"; the Ainu sometimes returned home without a penny.

Even today, lacquerware obtained as payment for labor or in trade exchanges with the Japanese can be found in Ainu homes. It is rarely known who received these and how, but the lacquer wine cup on a stand that Kaizawa Sirapeno had treasured until his death around 1940 is known to have been his payment for a year's labor in Atsukeshi in his youth. I later acquired this wine cup, now carefully preserved in a display case in the Nibutani Museum of Ainu Cultural Resources.

6. *Kinsei Ezo jinbutsushi,* written in 1854–1859, was censored by the Edo government and not published until 1969.

4

Following Forced Evacuation

THE AGE OF AFFLICTION for the Ainu, described in the preceding chapter, was to continue through the end of the Edo period and into the Meiji and Taishō eras, albeit in a different form. There are many sad stories from those days, but let me record just one.

The Saru River divides into two streams at Nioi, upstream from Nibutani. The left is the Saru River's main stream, and the right is called the Nukabira River. When you follow the Nukabira River upstream, you come to Nukibetsu. At Nukibetsu the river divides again, the main stream on the left and the Nukibetsu River on the right. If you go on along the Nukibetsu River a fair distance toward the upper reaches, you find terraced hills. The farthest of the hills is Kaminukibetsu.

Kaminukibetsu, located about 48 kilometers from the mouth of the Saru River, is deep in the mountains and quite high. Spring arrives there later than in Biratori and Nibutani, and the autumn frost comes two weeks earlier. The soil is arid and unsuitable for farming. Since the water level of the river is low, salmon are not known to swim upstream to the area. Yet some Ainu live there. Why would they live in a place so ill favored by nature?

In the Meiji era many *shamo* came over to Hokkaidō searching for good farmland. In the Hidaka area, they set their sights on the Niikappu and Shizunai, bountiful rivers with plenty of salmon swimming upstream; there are also many deer in the surrounding mountains. The climate, moreover, is mild, making the regions ideal for human habitation. Thus, as in the Saru River basin, highly populated Ainu villages dotted the riverbanks.

But influential *shamo* entered the area and designated it the pastureland of the imperial family of Japan. The Ainu who had inhabited the land from long ago became an "obstruction" in making the imperial pastures. Plotting to evacuate the Ainu, *shamo* officials chose Kaminukibetsu in the mountainous upper reaches of the Saru River. The deception by which they accomplished their goal was to install a horse-wagon route, or "horse railway" as it was called then, between Nioi and Kaminukibetsu, to make the latter appear a convenient location.

The distance from Niikappu to Kaminukibetsu is only a day's walk across the mountains and along the upper stream of the Atsuga River, but the two areas are worlds apart in terms of climate and soil. The Ainu could not comprehend being told to move from the fertile region they had inhabited for generations to a barren land. But there was no way to prevent the overwhelmingly powerful *shamo* from forcing the reluctant Ainu out of Niikappu. Some moving fees were subsidized, I am told, but the amount was minuscule.

The history of the Kaminukibetsu Primary School suggests that the evacuation of the Ainu from Niikappu and its vicinity was completed prior to 1916. According to the town history of Biratori, the school was founded in 1916. An examination of the origin of this school reveals that the entire village was moved here. Kaminukibetsu Primary School, the record shows, was established in April 1902 in Niikappu Village as the Anesaru Basic Education Institute. Five grades were instituted in April 1909, and in July of the same year, sewing was added. The following April, the institute became a "normal school" (the prewar appellation for an elementary school). Finally, in March 1916, a new school building was completed in Kaminukibetsu; its opening ceremony was held in April.

In Kaminukibetsu there is an old man who moved from Niikappu as a child. He is seventy-two-year-old Fuchise Saichirō. He believes that he was perhaps five years old when, seated in a *sintoko* attached to the side of a pack saddle on a horse, he traveled from Niikappu. The larger *sintoko*, or lacquer vessels from the Japanese mainland, were roomy enough to carry a child easily.

With him were his family of grandparents, parents, and five other children—sixteen people including Saichirō. When they arrived at what they were told was their land, they found numerous red elms so large that two adults could not encircle one with their arms outstretched. In those days red elms were considered useless, and no one wanted them, even for free. No one would buy them, and they were too thick for anyone but a woodcutter to saw up.

Saichirō's parents found a small space between several large trees, and once they had put up a *mun ewkaomap* (a teepee-shaped grass hut) for shelter from the rain and dew, they started to cultivate the land. Their first project was to build big fires here and there at the bases of the red elms to burn them down over the course of several days. Day after day, they tended fires "huge enough to broil a horse on a spit." They started farming the land they had thus cleared and expanded it from year to year, finally able to harvest two different kinds of millet.

With the amount of heavy labor they did, though, they could not raise enough to sustain themselves: First the grandfather became ill, then the father, then the mother and several children. They had tuberculosis, which in those days was as good as a death sentence. Still, they commuted 32 kilometers to the hospital in Biratori. Sometimes they went on horseback, but most often they walked; that distance was too demanding for the sick to return home on foot within the day.

Despite treatment, Saichirō's family lost its working hands one by one. His grandfather, father, mother, and several brothers died one after another, leaving only one adult—his totally sightless grandmother. It was then that young Saichirō's cruel struggle for life began.

Many of his neighbors who had also been driven out of Niikappu met similar fates. That was an era when no such system as welfare existed; if people were hard pressed, they were truly hard pressed. And trying to live on too little food, they died from malnutrition. Not one family could extend a helping hand to Saichirō's.

In the severe winter, Saichirō and his grandmother somehow survived on the sparse supply of millet in the house and potatoes from the earthen storeroom, but when the grasses grew back in the spring, the boy could not tell which kinds were edible. So he plucked all kinds of grasses and brought them to his blind grandmother. She felt each plant, then smelled it, telling him which were edible and which were not.

When he came back with a quantity of those kinds she had pronounced edible, she would touch each one carefully once again and finally let him stew them. Blinking her unseeing eyes, she felt each blade, and if even one stalk of a different kind was mixed in, she would separate it from the rest as if she had eyes in her fingertips. In the heap of grass to be cooked, Saichirō never found a single wrong blade. Besides wild grass, she had Saichirō bring sculpins, loaches, and crawfish from a stream, and cooked them in soup or broiled them.

From spring to summer, Saichirō, with his grandmother's guidance, gathered wild plants and caught various small fish for sustenance, keeping millet and potatoes for later planting. For days on end, they did not eat a single grain of rice. His eyes filled with tears, Saichirō told me that had it not been for their grandmother, he and his brothers would have starved to death.

Shishido Yoshi, who was also forced to move from Niikappu to Kaminukibetsu, had a similarly difficult experience. She moved with her husband, but he became ill soon after the birth of a baby, so she worked alone. One day their grass hut caught fire and burned down, leaving nothing—not even the baby's diapers. She devised a substitute for the diapers by heating butterburr leaves over a fire until they softened.

Both Saichirō and Yoshi observed that had they stayed in Niikappu, they would neither have lost their families nor experienced such hardship in their daily lives. They sighed deeply; the *shamo* had indeed imposed difficulties on them. Today only two or three Ainu families remain in Kaminukibetsu. The others died out or fled and thus scattered.

Let me return to my grandfather Totkaram here. This story was also passed along to me by my grandmother Tekatte: My grandfather had such a booming voice that the neighbors called him *haweruy ekasi* (strong-voiced old man), but he was not necessarily eloquent. He was a rather skilled hunter, however, often coming home with a bear or deer. He was also exceptionally adept at making arrows and took great pride in owning an iron arrowhead. When he hunted, he always carried that iron arrowhead with him, drawing it from his quiver only as a last resort. He considered it the soul of the quiver.

One day Grandfather went to the mountains to hunt bear. He came upon a bear with a yearling cub and killed the mother. The cub, however, climbed a tall pine nearby and would not come down. Young though it was, it weighed perhaps 75 kilograms and was covered with fluffy fur, so it looked quite large. It clung to the trunk near the top of the tree where there were few branches, and circled round and round. The cub was a bit beyond the range of a bamboo-tipped arrow.

My grandfather took out his precious arrow with the iron arrowhead and, aiming carefully, shot at the bear cub. The arrow went clear through the bear and embedded itself in the tree. The cub fell to the ground, but the iron arrowhead—which my grandfather valued next only to his life in importance—remained lodged at an angle near the top of the tree.

At a loss, Grandfather left the two bears and started climbing the tall tree in order to retrieve his treasured arrowhead. Grabbing the trunk with one arm and holding a *makiri* (knife) in the other hand, he at last carved out the arrowhead. The early Meiji, I understand, was a time when iron implements were so hard to come by that no one would have questioned taking such a risk for an arrowhead.

Still on the topic of hunting, I once heard that my grandmother Tekatte was accidentally hit by a trap arrow and fainted. When she was young and unmarried, she went to the mountains with some friends. As she led them along a single trail through a thicket, a trap arrow popped on her right. Thinking the poison arrow had pierced the back of her thigh, she fell in a dead faint. Since trap arrows were coated with enough poison to kill a savage bear, a timid person was likely to faint just on hearing them triggered. No wonder that my grandmother, who believed that the arrow had actually hit her, lost consciousness.

Some time later, she came to as her friends called her name. Upon examining her, they found that the poison arrow had pierced the back of her deerskin garment at thigh level but fortunately not even scratched her body. If set by skilled hunters, trap arrows never hit humans, because they were made to snap when the leg of a bear or deer was caught by a string attached to it. The string had a leeway of 30 centimeters, so if a woman walking with a normal stride touched it with her foot, the released arrow would fly behind her, as the human body is not wide enough to get hit.

Grandmother used to say that the time the trap arrow pierced the back of her cloak and when she first heard the snorting of horses as she camped out on the way to Atsukeshi were the two most terrifying experiences of her life.

I would like to digress a little to comment on the deerskin garment that was pierced by the trap arrow. People today may imagine deerskin as something terribly expensive. In my grandmother's youth, however, it was everyday wear for Ainu, as cotton clothing was not yet available. The garment was not a long robe reaching the ankles but a short cloak that just barely hid the knees and opened easily, since it lacked the overlapping front flaps kimonos have.

Deerskin robes were made by first flaying the hide of a deer and dumping it in the latrine to steep. It was pulled out after a week, taken to the mountain, and washed again and again, with creek water being poured over the hide as it was repeatedly stamped upon. It would of course have been easier to wash the hide in a river, but the Ainu never washed soiled objects in running water, which was considered sacred. After several washings, the hair fell away completely, resulting in the soft, tanned skin similar to what people use nowadays to wipe their eyeglasses. The skin was then sewn into a garment. Now that I think about it, it certainly does seem a luxurious costume.

I would like to note a few things about Ainu names. At present, our names are no different from ordinary Japanese names, but long ago they were unmistakably distinct. My grandfather's name was Totkaram, and my grandmother's name Tekatte. There were no surnames at first, but around 1872, when the Japanese created family registers, my grandfather was given the surname Kaizawa.

As I am sure the reader has already noticed, many people in Nibutani are called Kaizawa. This does not mean they are all related by blood; more often than not, they are unrelated.

There is a reason behind this. The government official who came to the area in the early Meiji to distribute surnames for the family registers was a heavy drinker who passed his time imbibing at the inn instead of doing his job. As the deadline approached, he had to hastily name the Ainu and apparently did so in the following fashion: "I see; so this village is called Pirautur [now Biratori]. Then let's name the Ainu here Hiramura [Pira village]. Next is Niputani [now Nibutani], so their name should be Nitani. What's the village beyond? Pipaus? What's *pipa*? I see; it's 'shellfish.' And *us*? So it means "'there is,' does it? Well then, let their name be Kaizawa [shellfish stream]." That is why many Biratori Ainu in the vicinity of the Saru River have the surnames Hiramura, Nitani, or Kaizawa. In none of these three cases do the names have anything to do with blood relations.

5

A Long Absence from School

As I described in the preceding chapter, we Ainu have a history of sorrow, but I spent my childhood ignorant of such a past. I finally entered Nibutani Primary School in April 1933—"finally" because I was in fact eligible to enter school in the Bihoro school district in Kitami in northeast Hokkaidō, where my adoptive family, the Kayanos, had moved.

When a notice of school entrance didn't show up from the village office as the new school year approached, my mother went to check with the school. Told that I was not registered in the village, she pleaded with them to let me start school with the others, promising to get my birth certificate as soon as possible. They accepted me without fuss, merely reminding her to deal promptly with the certificate.

I don't remember the entrance ceremony, but I have a vivid memory of the first day I went to school with my books and pencils. Kaizawa Fukuji, a boy two years ahead of me who lived across Osatsu Creek, stopped by to invite me along. My family could not afford a new schoolbag, so I left with several notebooks in my older brother's sailcloth bag with a shoulder strap. Though originally white, the bag had aged to a deep brown. Fukuji took my hand in his as I started out with the discolored bag; then later, noticing that I was carrying it on the wrong shoulder, switched it for me.

There were only two teachers at Nibutani Primary School: the schoolmaster, Fujii Daikichi, and the teacher, Hosaka Hitoshi. Schoolmaster Fujii taught first, fifth, and sixth graders in the same classroom, while Mr. Hosaka worked with second, third, and fourth graders.

On the playground was the miniature hall enshrining the venerable pictures of the emperor and the empress, along with a plaque of the educational edict. A cannonball, said to have been captured during the Russo-Japanese war, was mounted on a wall in the gym.

At the time I entered school, my clothes were hand-me-downs from my older brothers. Pupils from well-to-do families wore Western-style school clothes, but those from poor familes wore kimonos. Kimonos clothed at least one-third of the students.

It was the end of my second-grade summer. Nitani Sōzaburō from my class, Kaizawa Shōji in the first grade, and I stole a watermelon from Kaizawa Masao's field adjacent to the schoolyard. Passing right by the many fifth and sixth graders playing in the yard, we took the melon to the base of the Poromoi hill, cracked it open against a rock, and, sitting in a circle, ate the fruit. I didn't really have a sense of wrongdoing.

While we were eating, a recently retired teacher, Kuroda Hikozō, came over and said, "Boys, what possessed you to steal this watermelon? Come with me this minute." We followed him and were taken to Schoolmaster Fujii's official residence.

Mr. Fujii had not returned, so we waited for him, our small knees in a row. Since we were rarely allowed into the schoolmaster's residence, we looked around curiously and whispered to one another.

When he came back, we expected to be scolded roundly, but the dark-skinned schoolmaster entered the room with a smile, showing his white teeth.

"Shigeru, what happened?" he asked.

"Sir, we stole Masao Aca's watermelon."

Aca, short for *acapo,* means "uncle" and is a familiar term. Mr. Fujii laughed aloud, saying *aca* was funny. Then he sat upright and began talking:

"I hear that other kids saw you take Masao's watermelon and told Mr. Kuroda, and by the time he found you, you were already eating it. Masao has lots of children to feed, but instead of picking those melons, he was waiting for them to turn red. You boys took one before he could. From now on, you must never take something that belongs to another. Do you understand, Shigeru?"

He pressed me as the representative of the three. His words about Masao waiting for the melons to turn red so that he could feed his children pierced my heart.

But in third grade I committed a more serious transgression. I ate the currants from the bushes planted around the school in place of the usual hedge. The school tradition was to share those currants among the 100 or so students at the beginning of the second term after summer vacation. Those of us who lived nearby, however, had picked just a few currants at a time, nearly finishing them off before we knew what had happened.

On the first day of the second term, those who had eaten the currants were separated from the others to stand in a row to receive blows—slap, slap!—from the teacher's huge hand. Forty-five years later, I still can't forget that sound, that pain. Children today show no interest in either the currants or the gooseberries that I stole and ate as a child. Often when I see those deep red, small berries left on the ground, shriveling and turning black, I recall the past and burn with anger. I wonder at the lesson they planted with the berry bushes on the school grounds: Did they know the searing impression it would make on starved children?

I seem not to have a single happy memory from my poor school days. The family situation to which I had been oblivious in first and second grade became clearer to me by the time I was a third grader.

The athletic meet at Nibutani Primary was traditionally held on June 15. The flags of all nations were hoisted for the occasion. (In those days Nioi Primary, which was bigger than our school, didn't have international flags and always sent someone to borrow ours. Whenever we were taken to attend their meet, it was exciting to see our own school's flags fluttering in the sky.) As the date approached in my third-grade year, I worried about whether my parents would buy me the white shirt and pants worn on that day. Sometimes it seemed as if I couldn't expect my father and brothers, who worked some distance from the village, to send money home. Perhaps aware of this, my teacher took me aside and asked if money had arrived from my father. When I unabashedly answered, "It hasn't come yet," he told me to come to his house the following morning before all the others arrived at school. When I went there early the next morning, he handed me a sparkling white shirt and shorts. Maybe he had bicycled to Biratori the night before to buy them.

Either my father or brother had apparently brought home some money when I was a third grader, for I was finally able to have the white school cap I had wanted so much. I proudly wore it around the playground during noon recess on the day of the meet. A few friends had surrounded the well and were looking into it; I joined the circle. Way, way down, I saw my friends and myself in the white cap, reflected in the water.

As we were peering down, making noise and jostling one another, my friend T.'s hand accidently hit my cap. The cap fell deep into the well, landing in the water with an almost imperceptible splash. The reflection of our faces in the water became distorted and fragmented, and suddenly the children by my side all ran away.

It had happened in a flash. Left alone by the well, I remained staring at the brand new white cap, quietly sinking into the water. I knew I would be scolded when I got home.

My bitterest memory of primary school days is from the fourth grade. The day before school started, after summer vacation, the worn-out schoolbag containing my textbooks and summer homework was missing. I looked for it all over the house, searching every nook and cranny—which in our small house was no trouble—even loosening the floorboards to crawl underneath. My bag was not to be found.

On the first day of the fall term, the next day, I stayed home. I wanted to go to school, but I had neither textbooks nor my homework. Every day after that, I begged my mother to look for it. Having exhausted every possibility inside the house, she even went out to the fields in case a dog had dragged it there. Still, it was not found. Distressed, my mother asked Nitani Nari, a neighborhood woman who communicated with the gods, to try their wisdom, but the gods, too, were at a loss.

One day, after three months or so of this hunt, my mother dragged her unwilling son to school to explain the situation to the teacher. It must already have been November. It was decided that a friend would share his textbooks with me so that I could study. Once in the classroom, I found that I had fallen behind in my studies and could barely understand what was going on. Until then, I had been among the better students in class, but I began to lag and in the end found myself close to the bottom. I eventually started to feel reluctant about going to school and in fact began to play hooky. It was pretty much the same as not having gone to school in the second term of my fourth year.

One day close to New Year, when I returned from playing outside in the snow flurries, I saw the school sack, which I had as much as dreamed of, dumped by the fireplace. Blind with tears, I groped my way toward the fireplace and hugged the worn sack tight. When I wiped away my tears and checked inside the sack, I saw that nothing had been lost. I was filled with mixed feelings of attachment for and resentment toward the textbooks and summer workbook.

Choked with excitement, I asked my mother how the bag had been found and was stunned to hear that it was discovered in my grandmother's chest. By some kind of mistake, my grandmother had stored my bag away in it. Since she absolutely adored me, she could not have done it in order to give me trouble. Still, I could not hold back my tears, yet neither could I say one word of reproach to my grandmother.

I have never told this story to anyone. I thought talking about it would mean blaming Huci for my lack of fluency in Japanese and insufficient knowledge of its written system or, worse, bad-mouthing that gentle woman. I have recorded it here, however, because I can confirm to myself that my heart harbors no such ill will.

After that event I began to hate school and became withdrawn. Rather than trudging off to school, I chose to drop in on families looking for babysitters and play with the children. The adults knew I was playing hooky, but they found me handy and rewarded me by feeding me lunch. I played with the children until evening, and around the time my classmates were flocking off the school grounds, I hurried home.

This was how I became a "long-term absentee" from fourth to fifth grade. In the sixth grade, my interest revived, but by then it was too late. I graduated as a guest pupil, so to speak.

Ainu students constituted an overwhelming majority at Nibutani Primary School, and I have no recollection of being teased or bullied by *shamo* children for being an Ainu.

Researchers of Ainu culture and customs who have visited Ainu *kotan* in various parts of Hokkaidō often comment that Nibutani people are self-assured and open, and nonscholars agree. The reason can probably be traced to our childhood environment.

There is a saying, "A three-year-old's soul is carried to age 100" (As the boy, so the man). A growing blade of grass snipped in half either stops growing, becomes twisted, or sprouts in a different direction. So, too, humans are molded by their environment. A child who is bullied or victimized tends to become a timid adult.

Many Ainu in Hokkaidō attending predominantly *shamo* schools were bullied. Punning on Ainu and *inu,* the Japanese word for dog, was just the beginning: "Hey, look at the Inu!" Ainu children were also taunted that they were hairy, poor, and other things too painful to write down. For schoolchildren, the smallest thing can linger, the most trifling incident can hurt. Confronted by such treatment by the *shamo,* an Ainu child comes to hate school, develops a tendency to skip classes, falls behind academically, and in the end drops out. What kind of adults will such children grow up to be?

I have lately come to feel deeply that we Nibutani Ainu can be said to have spent a happy childhood in the sense that we were not targets of cruelty. Ainu students were in the majority at Nibutani Primary, for few *shamo* lived in the area. Among them were three men, each living alone. One of them, Ōmori, lived in a house atop the right side of Osat Slope,[1] closer to Biratori. He rented this house from an Ainu named Simonoa and seems to have been a woodcutter who made charcoal. He eventually became ill, and my mother and other neighboring Ainu took turns looking after him, but in the end he died.

---

1. Now Munro Slope, named after Neil Gordon Munro (1863–1942), a Scottish doctor who practiced in Japan and studied Ainu culture. He lived in Biratori from 1932 on. See Chapter 6.

The second was Sasaki Sakaru, nicknamed Kokko Sasaki by the villagers because he stammered. He lived near the Ōkawa River to the north of Nibutani Marsh and apparently recycled empty bottles. I don't remember how it came about, but I once slept in his bed. Before I knew it, I was asleep under his alcohol breath.

I don't know the name of the third man. He lived in the thickets on Kankan Slope, facing Nioi, in a hut with a roof made of straw mats and grass. He was about forty years old and always strained his ears at the slightest noise. There was something unpleasant about his constant nervousness; when I think back on it, he may have been a runaway from a labor camp or a prison. For some reason, he would take me to his shed, with its air of a secret hideout, and show me things he had stored away in the garret. "This is where I keep my valuables," he would say. Since this shed was by a stream branching off Ponkankan Creek and was completely invisible from the road, I think that other villagers were unaware of its existence. Before I realized it, both the shed and the man had disappeared.

Around 1935 hardly any jobs were available to Nibutani residents. My oldest brother, Katsumi, and my second brother, Yukio, were unable to complete their education at the primary school in front of our house, having been sent out to work before graduation.

My oldest brother worked as a live-in servant in the Fujimoto farmhouse in Yamamonbetsu (present-day Monbetsu). It was my task to go to Yamamonbetsu to get the money my brother earned. I am sure it was hard for him, but my job, too, was a demanding one for a third grader. I had to make the 18-kilometer trip on foot. Leaving Nibutani, I would pass Kohira, cross Apetsu Creek to the left of the Biratori bridge, and climb along Yurap Creek. Both sides of the trail, barely wide enough for a horse-drawn cart to pass, were covered by weeds and the branches of huge trees.

My parents were fully aware that this was no route to send a child my age on an errand, but they were hard pressed to make ends meet.

As the road narrowed and I no longer met anyone on the way, I would suddenly feel alone. I would recall the child assaulted by a bear in the *uwepekere* my grandmother had told me, and if the grass near me rustled in the wind, I would run in fright. As these scares recurred, I began to break into tears as I ran. Nevertheless, if someone suddenly appeared around a bend in the trail, I would hold back my tears and stop running.

High up the slope along Yurap Creek, a large tree blown down by the wind lay across the road. I would crawl under the tree to reach the pass. I didn't know the word *pass* then and used to think that it meant crawling under a toppled tree.

When I had finally crossed the terrifying pass and had reached the farmhouse where my brother worked, the Fujimotos handed me no more than 5 or 10 yen. Since rice cost 5 to 7 yen per bag in those days, even this small amount of my brother's earnings must have been a great help to my mother, who had to feed a large family, including me and my younger brothers.

My second oldest brother, Yukio, worked with my father at Furenai on the Tomiuchi rail line, which was in the opposite direction from and further away than Yamamonbetsu. It was 20 kilometers from Nibutani. That trip was another unpleasant chore. There was no pass to negotiate, but there was a house with a ferocious dog at a place called Pirikawakka, between the present Horokeshi Station and the Furenai graveyard. My fear of the dog made me abhor the trip. The dog may have barked at me simply because it was puzzled by a dirty Ainu child in tattered clothes, but I was agonizingly afraid that it would bite me. On my way back from Furenai, my father or brother was usually able to arrange for me to ride on the luggage rack of a chromium mining truck.

Because I knew too well that not only my father but my adolescent brothers worked hard to support my mother and the rest of us, I wanted to graduate from school quickly and go out to work for money. In those days I used to admire the foremen—the contractors who brought money and asked my father or brothers to work for them and the master woodcutters who worked in the mountains. "When I grow up, I'm going to be a foreman," I resolved in my child's mind, making that my single goal in life.

One winter, around 1935, relief programs were initiated in order to help jobless Nibutani villagers. Work consisted of spreading pebbles on a newly opened road (the present National Highway 237). The workers collected pebbles at the Saru River and carried them on their backs in a box the size of a large orange crate. I don't know how much they made from a day's work, but my brothers labored along with other villagers in the cold from early in the morning until late at night. Even once they were at home, they would make boxes for transporting pebbles or busily dry clothes soaked from carrying the pebbles.

At Nibutani Primary School, which I then attended, they distributed one rice ball each for lunch to pupils of poor families. As I remember it, this was not every day but once or twice a week. I don't think the program lasted very long either. I didn't like that we poor children received rice balls when other children brought their own lunch boxes from home, so I skipped school on days the rice balls were given out or, casting glances at the food, went home to slurp on millet gruel. Such a miserable experience with rice, I thought, was not for me.

Around that time, however, the oldest of my little brothers, Gensuke, became sick and gradually weakened. Thinking he might recover if he ate refined rice free of other grains, I went to school on the day they handed out rice balls. When I came home with what until then had been the object of my spite, my brother smiled at the sight of the snow white rice ball, but he no longer had the energy to eat it when I brought it near his mouth.

In the end my brother died. I think he was four or five. As my mother sewed the dark brown linen kimono he would be buried in, she said tearfully, "How happy Gensuke would have been if I

Millet is pounded with an iyuta, *a large wooden pestle. The women sing while grinding the sheaves of grain.*

had sewn a new kimono like this while he was still alive. What's the use of such a nice thing after he's dead?"

My mother was profoundly religious and put up many itinerant monks, such as those who passed by our house during their winter training, those who carried Nichiren sect drums,[2] and those who held priestly staffs. Sometimes she invited those guests in after we had already gone to sleep. She would pull our futons out from under us as we slept and spread them out for the monks. Every once in a while, then, we children woke in the morning to find ourselves lying only on the straw mattress.

My mother did not limit herself to putting up monks; she welcomed any passing travelers who were in distress. She barely had the time or money to help others but apparently thought that if a traveler died because she denied his needs, she would suffer lifelong punishment.

My mother often said that although the gods were invisible, they were everywhere, that they watched us even when humans did not, and that we should never steal or do bad things. Our house may have been full of holes, but my mother's all-encompassing love didn't have any gaps, not even the size of a pinprick. Her principle in bringing us up was to teach us to be *aynu nenoan aynu,* humanlike human beings.

---

2. The Nichiren sect was founded by the thirteenth-century militant prophet Nichiren. It remains one of the largest Buddhist sects in Japan.

6

My Father's Arrest

BEFORE I ENTERED SCHOOL, something terrible happened to my father—or, rather, to our entire family.

One day, a policeman with a shiny sword opened the wooden door to our house and entered, curtly saying, "Seitarō, shall we go?" My father prostrated himself on the wooden floor like a spider, the flat-bellied kind that hides in a flat nest, and answered, "Yes, sir." As he calmly looked up at the policeman, big teardrops rolled down his face.

My father was being arrested for salmon poaching. The salmon he caught every night to feed us brothers, the old women in the neighborhood, and the gods, were off-limits at the time.

When someone said, "He's going to be taken to jail," I only vaguely imagined a jail to be a tiny, tiny room where you couldn't stand upright because your head would hit the ceiling, and where you thus had to keep your knees bent.

My father left the house and walked toward Biratori with the policeman. "You can't go, Dad. Don't go!" I yelled, running after him. When I caught up with him, I grabbed his giant hands and screamed, "You can't go. What'll we eat if you go?" The adults who had come up from behind caught hold of me, and saying, "Don't cry; he's coming back right away," burst into tears themselves. Sobbing, I followed my father over a kilometer past Nibutani Primary School and through Nupesanke Field. Hurried along by the policeman, my father rapidly outpaced me, even as he kept looking back. I lay down in the road and wailed at the top of my lungs but was finally taken home, carried in turn on the backs of my mother and some neighbors.

At home my grandmother's grief was immense. The police, she charged, took her son for no reason; the arrest was unjustifiable. Later recalling her sorrow, she expressed it in the following words:

Sisam kar pe cep ne wa he, kupoho uk wa kamuy eparoyki koetu-renno, poho utar ere p akopak hawe ta an, wen sisam utar ukhi anak somo apak hawe ta an.

It's not as if *sisam* created salmon. My son caught salmon, offered some to the gods, and at the same time fed his children. Why is he punished for this? The wicked *sisam* are not punished for their catch—I cannot understand this.

Believing the adults who comforted me with the claim that my father would soon return, I went outside every day and gazed in the direction of Biratori, leaning against the wooden wall of our house. As the days passed, however, he did not return, and whenever I asked my mother when he would come back, her face clouded over and she would not answer.

One reason the Ainu had survived is that we got enough food, which for us meant salmon and venison. The Ainu treated salmon carefully, catching them only according to the providence of nature. Between September and October, when salmon migrated upstream to spawn, we caught only the amount we needed for that day's food. (Even if we had wanted to catch enough to preserve, salmon in this season were too fatty to preserve well.)

My father was arrested for fishing during the pre-spawning season. The Ainu knew, however, that the number of salmon would not be depleted in the wide Saru River by us. Spreading fishnets the width of an adult's outstretched arms and the length of two adults' arms extended, we only caught enough to feed our families. It was in fact the *shamo*'s indiscriminate fishing that caused the decrease in salmon around that time. The *shamo* were in essence blaming the Ainu for a problem they themselves had created.

We caught a large amount of salmon to preserve for winter only after spawning, when they turned white and their tails became broom-shaped[1] or the size of a baby's fist. Salmon are lean then; even when they are split open lengthwise and aired outdoors, they don't attract flies. The taste of such salmon is somewhat inferior, but they are still perfectly edible after a year or two.

The Ainu followed the laws of nature, skillfully applying their wisdom not only to catching salmon but also to trapping deer, bear, and other animals. Precisely because we were a hunting people, the Ainu had the wisdom and love that kept us from exhausting natural resources. The *shamo* law banning salmon fishing was as good as telling the Ainu, who had always lived on salmon, to die. For our people, this was an evil law akin to striking to death a parent bird carrying food to its unfledged babies. Other laws, such as the infamous Former Hokkaidō Aborigine Protection Act of 1899 (still in effect at this writing), also are nothing but expressions of *shamo* discrimination toward the Ainu.[2]

We are no "former aborigines." We were a nation who lived in Hokkaidō, on the national land called Ainu Mosir, which means "a peaceful land for humans." The "Japanese people"[3] who belonged to the "nation of Japan" invaded our national land. Ainu Mosir beyond a doubt was a territory indigenous to the Ainu peo-

1. A reference to salmon tails worn or shredded from rubbing during spawning.

2. The act defined Ainu as imperial subjects and the mission of the Japanese state as civilizing them. Ignoring the Ainu fishing and hunting traditions, the law allotted each family 5 hectares of land and pressed them to become farmers.

3. The author's quotation marks. He differentiates between Japanese people (Nihonjin) as a nation and mainlander Japanese (Wajin) as a people.

ple. Not only are the high mountains and big rivers graced with Ainu names, but so, too, is every creek and marsh, no matter how small.

Mainland Japanese had crossed the strait to our national land hundreds of years earlier, but it was in the early Meiji era that they began a concerted, all-out invasion. Laws like the Former Hokkaidō Aborigine Protection Act restricted our freedom first by ignoring our basic rights, as a hunting people, to hunt bear and deer or catch salmon and trout freely, anywhere and any time, and then by compelling us to farm on the inferior land the Japanese "provided." In "providing" land, the Japanese also legitimated their plunder of the region. The mountains around Nibutani, among others, became the Japanese nation's "national forests" before we realized it and later were sold off to a big financial combine.

This makes for an unqualified invasion. I have no knowledge of the usual methods by which strong countries invade weaker ones. There is no denying, however, that the people belonging to the "Japanese nation" ignored the rights of the Ainu, the prior inhabitants, and—without so much as removing their soiled shoes—stormed into Ainu Mosir, the land of the Ainu. If the "Japanese people" borrowed rather than invaded the land of the Ainu, there ought to be a certificate of lease; if they bought it, there ought to be a certificate of purchase. Since, moreover, that would have meant a contract between two states, the witness of a third country would have been desirable. Yet I have neither seen such a certificate nor heard of a witnessing country. This is perhaps a crude rendering, but in simple terms we have no recollection of selling or lending Ainu Mosir to the Japanese state.

Anyway, my father was forced to become a "criminal." The tears he shed then, I think, represented the Ainu people's tears of mortification. A conversation I had with my father comes to mind in relation to the word *criminal.* I reproachfully asked him later why he had given me, a child born a Kaizawa, away to the Kayano family for adoption. He answered, "You were a promising child, so I gave you to the family my older sister married into. Thanks to that, you never had to endure being called a criminal's child or an ex-convict's son." I listened to this explanation half in doubt, but perhaps he really had thought along these lines when he gave me up for adoption.

I have few pleasant memories of my father. He was a heavy drinker, did not get along with his wife, and rarely worked. He was born in 1893 to Kaizawa Totkaram and Tekatte and named Seitarō. He was the younger brother of three sisters, Utaasika, Umo-simatet, and Umon, and graduated in 1902 from Nibutani Primary School (founded in 1892) as a member of the fourth class. This was a time when Japanese-style education was in fashion, and the language was taught emphatically at school. My father thus led a double linguistic life, using Japanese at school and Ainu at home.

According to Nitani Zennosuke, who graduated from Nibutani Primary School in 1908, one child who had difficulty learning Japanese could not tell the teacher he wanted to go to the bathroom and so passed water on the floor, bursting into tears. Another had trouble counting in Japanese, and when the teacher swore "Idiot!" at him, the child echoed back "Idiot!" thinking it a number. There were many other humorous episodes I find it hard to laugh about.

For several years after completing his four years of compulsory education, my father helped my grandfather hunt and farm. He then went to Sakhalin, an island north of Hokkaidō, to hunt bears with a neighbor, Kaizawa Tetsuzō. Never successful there, he kept postponing his return and ended up staying in Sakhalin until he was twenty, when he had to submit to a physical examination for the draft.

Passing with a top grade, he joined the Twenty-fifth Regiment of the Tsukisappu Infantry. Perhaps because he could read and write to some extent and, as a member of a hunting people, had keen reflexes, he appears to have done fairly well as a soldier.

"In sumō wrestling I was first or second in the Twenty-fifth Regiment, and I received a good-conduct commendation when I finished my two years of military service"—this was his claim, unless I misheard. To this boast my father always added, "If you don't believe me, go to Biratori and ask Hiramura Ichirō, who enlisted with me."

After his arrest for poaching around 1932, however, my father gradually became addicted to alcohol. Working less and less, he supported his drinking by selling my grandfather's horse, then even the storehouse my grandparents had toiled to have built. For 20 yen he let our next-door neighbor Kaizawa Seihachiro take the storehouse that had once brimmed with unthreshed millet. My grandmother cried as she watched it being pulled to the next lot as a result of her son's wretched plight. By the time I was old enough to remember things, Kaizawa Ukichi lived in that building.

The storehouse was built by the Japanese carpenter Arita Asajirō, who came in 1911 to remodel Nibutani Primary School. The storehouse stood on a foundation (Ainu buildings have none) and measured 5.4 by 7.2 meters. Several other people also had Arita build storehouses. I remember seeing four as a child: Nitani Kunimatsu's, Kaizawa Motokichi's, Kaizawa Uesanasi's, and my grandfather's. There may have been others. Arita settled with his family in Nibutani, and I recall seeing them in my youth.

Another settler I remember from my childhood is Neil Gordon Munro, a naturalized Japanese and medical doctor who lived in Nibutani from 1930 to 1942 to research Ainu culture. When I once led my grandmother by the hand to his place for a visit, he told me, "Your father Seitarō is a good man, but unfortunately he drinks. Liquor is *wen kamuy* [evil god]. You mustn't drink when you grow up, Shigeru." Young as I was, I vowed to myself that I would never become a drinker.

My father had married a young Nibutani woman before his marriage to my mother. Because she did not bear him a child, he divorced her and married my mother. My mother, Hatsume, was born on May 14, 1899, as the second daughter of Monbetsu Suke-roku of Yamamonbetsu in Monbetsu Village. She married Seitarō unaware of his heavy drinking, discovering only later that he drank instead of working. She spent her days thinking, "I'll go home to my parents today" or "I'll run away tomorrow," but then she had my oldest brother. Soon, my second oldest brother came along, then me, and thus, she once reminisced, she continued to live with my father, unable to leave.

What was my father's occupation? He was fond of hunting and frequently engaged in it but never made a living at it. He said he had caught fourteen bears in Enbetsu (in Teshio in northern Hok-kaidō) and in Sakhalin, but I never saw him capture one.

He often set weasel traps that we were responsible for checking. "This morning, a weasel should be in the trap at such and such a place, so go there quickly," he would say, and when we ran there, making our way over the crunchy frost, we always found a weasel. When asked how he knew, my father would answer with a laugh, "The gods whisper to me in secret." Later, he revealed, "Actually, I knew it from my dreams. Whenever I dream about a guest, espe-cially a female one, visiting us, a weasel is sure to be trapped."

The best bait for catching weasels was eel and sculpin, found under the thin ice of small creeks in late autumn. Weasel pelts sold for 2 or 3 yen apiece around 1935. Since ten cups of rice cost 20 to 25 sen around that time, weasel hunting helped our livelihood somewhat.

When the snow flurries started, my father set rabbit traps. Checking them was also my responsibility. The device, *hepitani* (popping wood), was made of brushwood about 2 meters long and 4 centimeters wide at the root. Its stem was inserted deep into the ground wherever rabbits were likely to pass, and its top was bent and a wire trap loop attached. At a height of about one adult fist above the ground, the loop was gently hooked to a stake pounded into the ground. When a rabbit was trapped in the ring, the top of the brushwood sprang free, lifting the rabbit by the

Hepitani *(rabbit trap)*

forelegs. If the brushwood sprang up with too much force, the entire rabbit would be raised in the air and break the trap loop. The
optimum strength was when the rabbit could barely wriggle
around with its hind legs on the ground.

One aspect of flaying the rabbit required special attention. Rabbits have little subcutaneous fat. At the root of each front leg, however, there is a tiny lump of fat the size of the tip of a little finger.
With pomp, my father held out the small lump in both hands,
bowed two or three times, and prayed, "O god of the rabbit,
thanks be to you for bringing us much fat meat." This was so that
the god of the rabbit would be flattered and, taking the words seriously, would send rabbits again and again to that Ainu family.
Good-for-nothing idler that he was, my father was still a member
of the hunting people.

The rabbits were either to be eaten right away stewed, or boiled
and dried for preservation. The head was stewed whole, except
the eyes. After the scanty meat on it was neatly removed, the head
was prepared to look like a live rabbit's: The skull was decorated
with beautiful *inaw* (whittled willow twigs with curled shavings
left attached, important ritual objects), eyes of rolled *inaw* were
inserted, a tongue was attached, and long ears were made to stand
at pert attention. The rabbit head was hung for a while at the win-

dow near the master's seat in the main wing of the house and later taken outside to the altar, to be sent back to the land of the gods.

Around 1935, when my father returned from a hunting trip to Enbetsu in Teshio, we watched as he pulled numerous *hecaweni* from his bags. *Hecaweni* is the trap portion of a trap bow for shooting bears. With this and an arrow, he could lay a trap in the mountain at a moment's notice—all he needed was to cut out material for the bow. These were the first *hecaweni* I had seen.

Besides hunting, my father worked in the mountains as a woodsman, or mountain boy as it was traditionally called in Japanese. He was skilled in the use of a special ax for planing railroad ties and wood for houses. At various times he worked at processing timber, making tracks for transporting timber out of the mountains, and so forth.

In the spring around 1938 or 1939, he went to the Kuriles to work for a fishing company. Before his departure, in late February or March, the foreman gave him an advance of 50 or 100 yen. My father used the money for food and drink, then set out for the Kuriles in May after the snow thawed. He returned by late September without bringing home much money.

At that time, a fair number of Ainu were hired for this type of work. Recruiters would come, flashing bills for the advance, just when the Ainu were most financially strapped, between winter and early spring. Although times had changed and Ainu labor was somewhat compensated, I doubt there was much difference from the former days, when our grandfathers were compelled to work as slaves.

My father must have truly loved salmon fishing. Even after he had been arrested for poaching, he continued to catch salmon for us and our neighbors whenever he was home. Occasionally, the net caught a crab instead of a salmon. My father would lightly bind it with a cord, tie it to a willow tree, and tell it, "You are the river god's servant, so you should be able to communicate with the god. Ask the river god to make a gift of a salmon to this Ainu.

We, the Ainu, whom you can see, are not the only ones who eat the salmon. The invisible fire goddess and other goddesses share it with us. If no salmon is caught, both the Ainu and the gods suffer from hunger. Unless you talk to the gods so I catch a salmon, I won't untie the cord."

Strange as it may seem, once my father intoned this chant, he inevitably caught a salmon in the net. He then untied the crab and set it free in the river. Most Ainu usually gave up and went home when they caught crabs in the net. My father, who talked to this inauspicious creature, may in fact have had the power to speak to the gods.

Walking in the mountains, my father sometimes muttered without any context, as if suddenly remembering something: "In the old days, there was no such thing as a border between land and land. If I needed a tree, all I had to do was offer *inaw* and wine with a prayer—'This tree will be used for such and such a purpose; please give it to this Ainu.'"

He also taught me that when walking in the mountains, we were not to startle the god of the mountains by raising our voices or otherwise creating disturbances. "When you're walking by the river or the edge of a marsh, don't move a rock without reason," he said. "If you lift a rock to get fish bait, you're expected to put it back where it was." Now that I think back, I see that my father was imbued with the spirit of a hunting people.

He lived in poverty, however, because he was a heavy drinker and, moreover, was not fond of farm work. He was therefore only asked to play secondary or tertiary roles at important Ainu events. He was fully aware of this, and yet he could not keep himself from drinking every day.

In 1937 a visitor from Shizunai, the husband of my father's cousin from Kohira, Kaizawa Tomaat, drowned in the river. His body did not resurface, as the early spring thaw had increased the flow of water, and it was finally decided to hold the funeral without the body.

At a funeral where the corpse was missing, a doll that looked exactly like the deceased was made by stuffing his or her clothing with cattails. Once the doll was placed where the real body would have been, a little way down from the family head's seat to the right of the fireplace, a full funeral followed.

This man, Tsukimoto, was from Shizunai. In order to greet the many Ainu who would attend the funeral, Shishido Sansuke (Ainu name Yonke) of Kohira was selected as representative. After the first round of the reception, however, Sansuke gathered local leaders for consultation. "Just look how eloquent those Shizunai folks are," he said. "And there will be more of them tomorrow. This old man is no match for them. Please allow Kaizawa Seitarō of Nibutani to take charge of everything."

This was the first time my father faced Ainu from other communities as a village representative. I was a little boy then, and my father's excitement was exhilarating. I accompanied him to the funeral ceremony, called *uniwente*, the day after the wake conducted with the straw man.

An *uniwente* was not observed when someone died of illness; it was limited to marking deaths by unnatural causes. The word consists of *u* (mutually), *niwen* (to rage), and *te* (to cause), meaning "getting angry together." When, as in this case, someone drowns, for example, the Ainu scolds the god of the river: "We have a victim because you were slack. You must endeavor to prevent such accidents in the future." Or if someone is burnt to death in a fire, the Ainu reprimands the goddess of fire, and when a bear mauls someone to death, not only the god of bears but the god of the mountains is reproved. In our Ainu world, humans and gods are perfectly equal; we do not consider the gods to possess absolute power.

Near the altar built to the east of Kaizawa Tomaat's house in Kohira, the thirty or so guests from Shizunai lined up on the west; to the east, about forty locals welcoming them lined up, with the house between the two groups. Each group was formed of men

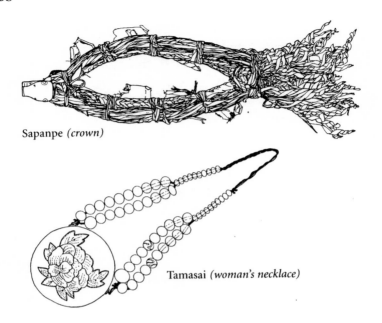

Sapanpe *(crown)*

Tamasai *(woman's necklace)*

first and women following. Leading each file were the village representatives responsible for offering greetings. My father thus stood at the front of the local participants.

Both men and women wore embroidered robes. Each man carried a sword from the shoulder, slung in front of the body. For funerals they did not wear the *sapanpe*, a decorative headband worn for ordinary rituals. The women wore bead necklaces called *tamasai* and covered their heads with 30-by-100-centimeter black cloths folded in two, tied once behind their heads and draped down the back. In their left hands they held staffs.

When both parties were ready, my father drew his sword and, holding it in his right hand, raised the cry, "Wohohoho hoohoy," as he took one step forward. The women responded with "Wooy," also taking one step forward. The men called "Wohohoho hooy"; the women answered, "Wooy." Exchanging these calls, they advanced to the altar, step by step.

As they neared the principal mourner, they halted and carried out *ukewehomsu*, "appreciation of each other's work," stamping the right foot with each word. My father stepped so firmly with each word, flexing and stretching his right hand as it held the sword, that his foot sank to the ankle in the dent it made in the earth.

Keeping time with his movements, the men behind stamped on the ground, thrusting their right hands and swords forward. The women, holding staffs in their left hands, thrust their right fists forward and let out piercing cries in time with the men. This was called *pewtanke*, a special form of vocalization. When in an emergency a woman used *pewtanke* with all her might, her voice could be heard 4 kilometers away. The women's movements, too, were powerful. Auntie Mone of Apetsu Creek, with a staff in her left hand, arched her body backwards and thrust her clenched fist forward so forcefully that she seemed to exude enough energy to chase off demons.

To each word my father chanted at the head of the line, the women responded with "*wooy.*"

Wakkauskamuy	The god of water	*wooy*
ekoro iwro ta	in your garden	*wooy*
tapan pe neno	in this manner	*wooy*
cikatuwente	shame	*wooy*
uan rok katu	has been experienced.	*wooy*

The narration went on and on in this fashion. This, in essence, is the *uniwente* funeral. Since the leader improvises according to circumstance, he must be fairly eloquent to fulfill the role. There was nothing to admire about my father in daily life, but on that day I felt that I could take a certain pride in his worthiness.

On the way home in the dark night, my father was in high spirits as he reviewed the day, lustily mimicking the Shizunai leader's chanting. Having just turned forty, he had proven himself a true Ainu orator, a *paweto*.

7

An Adolescence
Away from Home

I SHOULD BE WORKING instead of going to school, constantly lacking food and clothing—that was all I thought about while I was in school. In March 1939 I graduated from Nibutani Primary in its fortieth graduating class. My classmates from better-off families went on to secondary school in Biratori, but I had no desire to continue my education. Or, rather, I had probably suppressed all hope in the face of impossible odds.

On April 10, barely two weeks after graduation, I went to the workers' lodge in the mountains to plant trees. Using vouchers to buy rubber-soled workers' toe socks, a lunch box, and other items, I left home carrying my futon. I was twelve years old. Although children fresh from primary school could hardly be expected to contribute much in the mountains, five of us from the same class went together: Kaizawa Kenjirō, Kaizawa Keiji, Kaizawa Tsuneo, Nitani Sōjirō, and myself.

My first stop was at the Urakawa Forestry Office's work station, located in the upper reaches of Kankan Creek, not far from Nibutani. The station was housed in a long building, measuring 6 by 60 meters, with a single layer of thin boards for siding and a roof of red spindle-tree thatch. Running the entire length of the building at its center was a dirt floor, 2 meters wide, with thin straw mats placed along the walls on both sides. The tatami-sized mats served to mark off individual sleeping spaces. The two or three campfires that dotted the long dirt floor were tended by a few men drying wet belongings or warming themselves.

I was excited by the glorified status inscribed on what served as my letter of appointment: "Kayano Shigeru, forester for the Ura-kawa Forestry Office: 1.30 yen per day." The forestry officer who prepared those documents was Minai Ryōzo, known as "Boss" to the workers.

Our first job involved stepping on the soil around the saplings planted the previous fall. This was to firm up the soil that had frozen and risen during the winter, making the trees unsteady. Children our age were considered the ideal weight for this job. Lightly holding onto the pine saplings, grown to a height of almost 30 centimeters, we stamped with both feet on the soil above the roots.

My uniform consisted of a short kimono, a hatchet worn at the hip, mountain-work gaiters on the lower legs, and rubber-soled toe socks that were reinforced with shiny black enamel and smelled of new rubber. This was an outfit I had adored since childhood.

The workday was from 5:30 A.M. to 5:30 P.M. With a fifteen-minute break at 9:00, a one-hour lunch break, and another fifteen-minute break at 3:00, we worked ten and a half hours altogether.

They fed us white rice, which we greatly enjoyed, and miso soup that we dubbed "mirror soup" because we could see our faces reflected in the big bowl of clear broth. We were charged 27 sen a day for meals. We were to supply our own side dishes; they provided none. On the rare occasions when they did serve something, it was only miso paste. No wonder we workers lost our strength and health.

A man from my village by the name of Kaizawa Moheikichi became ill while working as a forester. His final words to his wife were, "I fell ill from planting in the mountains. Don't ever let our sons plant trees." I witnessed one son, Terumichi, disobey his father's deathbed injunction and sign up as a forestry worker, only to take sick and die.

Although I was only a child just out of school, I proposed that they add dried fish to improve the miso soup. Shredded dried bonito in those days cost 27 or 28 sen per package for the Treasure Boat brand with the picture of a leaping fish. I therefore calculated that we could afford it if each of the thirty workers paid an additional sen per day for food. Not one of the thirty adults listened to my proposal, instead berating me: "You're just a kid. Don't be so cocky."

The diseases that came with the job were pleurisy from malnutrition and tuberculosis of the lungs. If someone mentioned chest pains, the adults later whispered to one another: "That's it for him. It's TB." Back then, contracting tuberculosis was as good as receiving a death sentence. Then why not quit working here? I thought. For an adult Ainu, however, it wasn't as simple as that: Hungry children were waiting at home, and jobs weren't easily available at the time.

Frightened by the prospect of illness, I vowed not to stay in forestry work forever. Then something happened that only compounded my loathing for tree planting. Once we were finished tamping down sapling roots, we were told to plant seedlings. No matter what his age, each worker was given a quota of 350 seedlings a day. We children set out in the morning with 350 four- or five-year-old seedlings on our backs, the loads so much larger than we that it looked as if the seedlings had grown legs and were walking.

The forestry officers had sent us those seedlings with orders to plant 300 per 10 square meters. Unlike level land, however, the mountains were covered with rocks and big roots that made it impossible to plant in such numbers. The seedlings hopelessly outnumbered the spaces available for them.

Claiming that it was for fertilization, the adults began to dig deeper holes than necessary and, when the overseers weren't watching, buried two or three seedlings in each hole, planting just one on top. What a terrible waste, I thought, as they buried those healthy seedlings raised over a four- or five-year span.

When I attempted to plant my seedlings carefully, I was scolded by the adults. Besides, no matter how hard I worked, there seemed to be just as many seedlings as before in my bag. Seeing no other option, I gradually learned to sacrifice some seedlings as fertilizer. But my distrust of adults steadily increased, and I started to hate forestry work all the more.

After the planting I worked until autumn weeding under trees and, to help prevent fires, weeding the borders between privately owned and government-owned forests. I quit working in the forest after this stint in the summer of 1939.

In search of a job I could perform on my own, I became an apprentice woodcutter. My boss was Koishikawa Seikichi, my uncle by marriage, and we worked along the Hatonai Creek in the upper reaches of the Monbetsu River. Woodcutting allowed me to work in whatever manner and however much I pleased, so I truly enjoyed learning the trade. I started by cutting large logs, then learned how to sharpen saws and how to finish off trees. When a tree was to be cut at the roots, the lower part of the tree was shaved with an ax on the side it was to fall. This final rudiment of woodcutting that Seikichi taught me was called "getting ready" and meant just that.

My life as a woodcutter's apprentice lasted about one and a half years, from the fall of 1939 until the spring of 1941. I became quite adept at sharpening saws, but to this day I do not qualify as a full-fledged woodcutter.

During this interval I suffered a great loss. My second oldest brother, Yukio, died of tuberculosis on July 21, 1940. He had hardly ever gone to school but had labored to support the family and was never rewarded for his sacrifices. He was twenty-one.

In March and April of that year, I was unable to cut wood because of the snow in the mountains. With my older sister Toshiko, I went to work at a herring site, Rumoi, on the Japan Sea, far from Nibutani. This may sound as if we went to sea, but our work was processing fresh herring at the Kanebun Hashimoto factory located in the northern part of the port. My sister became ill and returned to Nibutani, but I worked the full term of my employment before going home. I was thirteen.

On my return I spent a month in the home of strangers, a *shamo* family on the marsh near our house. I paid for my room and board by rounding up their horses. The grandfather there was extremely nasty. At mealtimes, when I finished my first bowl of rice and was ready for a second, the old man would rise, holding a kettle of hot water. In a raspy voice he would say to his grandson who was my age, "N., how about some hot water to finish off our supper? Shall we have it now?" He would then pass the kettle to me. Since I was hungry, I would ask for a second helping, but a third was out of the question. The old man's kettle of hot water thrust aside my request before it could be voiced.

Day after day, his hoarse voice repeated, "N., some hot water? Hot water?" I grew sick of it and left for home. Although it had only lasted a month, I learned the discomfort of having to eat at someone else's table and resolved ever more firmly to become my own boss.

When I returned home in the spring of 1941, I heard the Hokkaidō government needed one more person for a land survey team. The job entailed entering virgin forests deep in the mountains to precisely mark the borders between government- and privately owned forests. Hearing that a wage of 1.80 yen would be paid just for showing up, even when rain stopped work, I gave up my woodcutting apprenticeship for good and became a surveyor. The team consisted of six people: Sugawara Isamu, a twenty-five- or twenty-six-year-old Hokkaidō government official who was also a second lieutenant from the military academy; a Murai; a Fujishima; a Fukushima; Sakamoto Santarō; and myself.

We went to a place called Nukanrai along the upper reaches of the Niikappu River. The area was one of pristine forests where no man had ever wielded an ax. Surveyors had to go on foot in those mountains, and we carried tents, provisions like rice and miso paste, and fishing poles to catch the river fish. Our guide was Sakamoto Santarō, an Ainu. Since he hunted from fall to winter in the mountains along the Niikappu upstream, he knew the terrain intimately. The villagers called him Santarō Acapo, Uncle Santarō.

Our job was to establish valley-to-peak or peak-to-peak lines, called forest-interior lines, in government-owned forests and to clear trails between those spots. We were to pound stakes and paint them red as survey markers and of course measure the areas of the government forests.

I worked as a surveyor for two summers, from May to October in 1941 and 1942—twelve months altogether. This proved a precious experience for me as an Ainu. I had previously learned things here and there from my father, but during those twelve months I received a firm grounding in the basics of Ainu hunting wisdom. Let me describe the lessons as they come to mind.

For one, Santarō Acapo taught me how to carry a large catch of trout. In late August many trout swim upstream to the upper reaches of the Niikappu River. The most efficient way to catch them is to start from the lower stream and climb upwards, placing the caught trout at the shallow edge of the water. Once you have as many as you need, you cut a wild grapevine and, on the way back, thread the fish one by one at the gills, pulling the vine behind you through the water. This way, you can carry thirty or forty trout yourself. If you carry them on your back, ten is the limit.

A trout that is digging in preparation for spawning swims away with a splash if you touch its back, but you can safely touch its underbelly. Wear cotton gardening gloves and, with fingers spread, place your hands under the belly of the trout, then scoop the fish through the air onto the shore.

Once they have spawned, in late autumn, the trout migrate in droves to the shallows. Bears do not eat the fish whole but lumber around, taking just one bite from each fish at the front of its head, just above the mouth and between the eyes, where there is soft bone and oil. The bears know there is fat only in that area of the trout after it spawns. (If you see many trout missing chunks from their heads, watch out for bears!)

When you camp out in the mountains, pine branches with needles are good for making a hut, as are butterburr leaves used with ferns and the bark of the katsura tree. Whether summer or winter, don't construct a camp hut where a tree has fallen downward on a slope. It means there was an avalanche in winter, and the area will be dangerous in rain as well.

When you and your friends are lost in the mountains and call out for one another, don't use real names like Santarō and Shigeru, as a monster may appear, disguised as Santarō or Shigeru. Instead, call out "Katchi-i, Katchi-i!" (*Katchi* is not an Ainu word but a special term mountain workers used to signal an area close to the peak at the source of a mountain stream.) I also learned such things as how to use the *marep*, a fishhook unique to the Ainu.

One day, Santarō Acapo took me to the hunting shed he used in the winter. It was located on the opposite side of the Nukanrai Stream; that is, on the left shore of the Niikappu River, and both the roof and walls were made of katsura bark. Adjacent to the hut stood a tall red elm with a hollow of approximately 1 meter at the base of its fat trunk. Santaro Acapo showed me the hollow and said, "If you're ever stuck without food, look inside this hollow. I've hidden several ten-cup bottles filled with polished millet. The

bottle openings are airtight, with melted wax to fend off damp-
ness. You'll be able to survive for several days at least."

He then went on: "I've shown you this because you're an Ainu. I
forbid you to tell anyone else about this." Feeling as if he had
taught me the principles, or perhaps the spirit, by which a hunting
people lived, I nodded with sincere gratitude. And I never had to
rely on Santarō Acapo's precious bottled grain.

I saw a brown bear[1] for the first time during the survey. On September 3, 1941, I was taking a nap after lunch with the head surveyor, Murai. He shook me awake, whimpering, "Shigeru,
Shigeru, there's a bear." As I sat up in disbelief, I saw a brown bear
standing upright, just 7 or 8 meters ahead and looking straight at
us, with one foreleg on the trunk of a pine tree.

Since we were working deep in the mountains, I knew there
were brown bears around, but I had never expected one to appear
before my very eyes. Bears usually run away at the sound of human voices and other noises, but because we were napping and
there were no sounds, the bear had not noticed us. He must have
stopped in bewilderment at finding strangers in his path.

My first thought was, "Look at that cute thing—it's just like a
sheepdog." The instant I reminded myself that bears are ferocious
animals capable of mauling us to death and eating us, I felt my
legs buckle (granted, I was seated, so it sounds odd, but ...).

Eventually, the bear, which had been casting a steady eye at us,
gently lifted its leg from the tree and padded off into the shrubs,
rustling against them. Murai and I remained trembling and
speechless for the longest time, then finally faced each other in relief, mutely reveling in the outcome. Although I worked in the

---

1. The brown bear inhabits north central areas of the Northern Hemisphere,
including Hokkaidō. It stands around 2 meters and is much larger and more ferocious than the bear common in other parts of Japan.

mountains for twenty years, from 1939 to 1959, this was my only encounter with a brown bear.

In that period as a surveyor, I heard the dismaying news that my oldest brother, Katsumi, had died. He passed away on September 27, 1941, but because I was in the mountains, I did not find out until mid-October. I was unable to be at his deathbed, just as when my second oldest brother died. Having lost their second son to tuberculosis in July of the preceding year, my parents lost their firstborn to the same disease a mere fourteen months later. How great their sorrow must have been to have two children go before them.

After passing the draft examination as an A-class soldier, Katsumi had joined the Seventh Regiment of Asahikawa in the summer of 1938 and was immediately dispatched to China. He contracted tuberculosis at the front, where he was stationed from 1939 until spring 1941, and was sent back to Japan. Despite medical treatment, he died at age twenty-five. With the deaths of their oldest sons, my parents decided that I would be the heir of the Kaizawa family, though remaining a Kayano in the registry.

Immediately following my oldest brother's death, my family decided to try charcoal making and, with the assistance of my brother's friend Satō Kikutarō, moved into the mountains along the Osachinai Stream. Our family finances were precarious because of the medical expenses for my brothers, and we were told that food would be provided if all of us worked together at charcoal making.

I worked as a surveyor in the summer of 1942 but, worried about my parents and little brothers producing coal by themselves, rejoined my family in the autumn, throwing myself into charcoal making. If I remember correctly, we received 1.25 yen for each 30-kilogram bundle of charcoal sold in straw bags. We made fifty bags or so worth of charcoal at each baking in a kiln measuring approximately 3.6 by 5.4 meters, but since we were able to load the kiln only twice a month, we earned just 130 yen or so. Even that amount represented great effort on our part.

We heard about the eruption of the "Great East Asia War" on December 8, 1941, while working at our kiln. We worked hard, urged on by such slogans as "Charcoal is indispensable for tempering cannons" and "The soldiers at the front in cold, cold Manchuria depend on the charcoal you produce."

The scent of war drifted as far as the charcoal makers' huts. Newspaper reporters back from mainland China, for example, came to tell us about Manchuria, and Marquis Ikeda inspected the kilns and encouraged charcoal makers. I was also called up to Furenai for military training several times. During one of many swimming drills, I remember watching a man named Sonoki Hideo drown.

Since we had gone to the mountains as a family, my grandmother Tekatte was with us. This meant I heard Ainu in daily use around me. Sometimes, when I was reading under the dim lamplight, my grandmother called my name and told me to listen to her *uwepekere*. "Sure," I answered loudly, for she had grown hard of hearing, and off she went. I was much more interested in reading than listening to her stories, so I listened halfheartedly with my book in hand and sometimes didn't even notice when she finished. At the end of a story, it was customary for the listener to express gratitude by saying *hioy oy* (thank you), and my grandmother used to scold me, lost in my book, for not thanking her.

Just before the winter of 1943, my youngest brother, Teruichi, barely one year old, ran a high fever in the middle of the night. The hospital in Biratori was 20 kilometers away, and in those days when there were no cars, it was by no means easy to travel along the pitch dark mountain trail. My father told me to cut down a pagoda tree so he could make an Ainu god. Rather than stand by helplessly watching his baby son die, he wanted to pray to the gods as a last resort. I took my next brother, Sueichi, then in primary school, to the dark woods to cut down a tree. It measured about 6 centimeters in diameter and 45 centimeters tall.

My father carved an icon out of the tree and an *inaw* out of willow then loudly prayed to that improvised god to cure Teruichi. Thanks, perhaps, to the god's protection, Teruichi's fever miraculously went down by morning, and he quickly regained his vigor. I believe the god answered my father's prayer because of his earnestness.

When she rose that morning my grandmother said she was concerned because—though it might have been her imagination—she thought she had heard *kamuy oroitak* (chanted prayers) from a distance the previous night. When my mother explained what had happened, my grandmother looked at Teruichi, now recovered, and said joyfully, "No wonder he's all better."

At Osachinai my father carried out one other characteristic Ainu act. One winter morning when we went as usual to the mountain to cut wood for charcoal, we found, scattered about, the saws and axes we had stored away the previous day. On investigating, we realized it was the work of a fox: Not only were there footprints in the snow, but narrow toothmarks were clearly visible on the tool handles.

My father wordlessly gathered dead branches and set them afire. When the branches started burning with red flames, he flopped down cross-legged near them and solemnly began *onkami,* a special form of Ainu worship. He placed his elbows against his sides with his arms stretched forward, palms facing inward and fingers outstretched. He rubbed his palms together, then turned them upward, slowly raising and lowering them as he prayed in Ainu. His prayer was to the goddess of fire sojourning in the bonfire in front of him:

Aynu ne yakka	An Ainu I,
kamuy ne yakka	in order to raise my children
	need what is called money;
urespa nemanup	so into the tranquil mountain
e pe ka kusu	I have entered to cut standing trees
kamuy iwor so	and harmed the divine mountain-
	dwellers' abode and garden

iwor so kasi	much to my regret.
koecatcari	But humans and gods alike
kuki sir	raise children.
oripak ram	I, too, have many children.
koyoyrap	In order to feed them
somo ne korka	and keep them from hunger
kikir koinne p	I must come to the highest mountain to work
kune wa kuiki sir ine na	Oh god
iteki iruska wa	think of this
enkore yan	and permit an Ainu's deed.

In closing, he continued, "You scattered an Ainu's tools like this, I think, in order to reveal secretly, just to the Ainu, an omen of change. Today I will stay away from work and repent, so please protect us." As he talked, he collected the scattered tools and, carrying them on his back, promptly returned to the charcoal-burning hut. The Ainu called the ransacking of tools and temporary hunting sheds in the mountains by foxes *kamuy ipirima*, "gods' whisperings." Considering these omens divine warnings, we cautioned one another against the danger they could foretell. Soon after this event, the roof of a nearby charcoal-burning kiln belonging to the Ogawas caught fire. Both roof and kiln burned down. My father said nothing but looked knowingly at us.

In the autumn of our charcoal-burning days, we ran from the far end of the Osachinai Stream to the big river to catch salmon; in winter we trapped rabbits and shot pheasants with guns. If ever we lived as members of a hunting people, it was in this period. The charcoal burning, however, proved fruitless. Although the entire family worked hard, covered with soot, we never made any money. I suppose our earnings were cleverly siphoned off by our boss and others. I grew sick and tired of charcoal burning.

We were not the only ones suffering; every charcoal burner was in the same straits at the time. My family was actually better off than many. Those who had grown up in the charcoal business had always lived in charcoal-burning huts without ever being able to call a place their home. "You're so lucky. You have a home to go back to," they would tell us enviously.

In October 1944 we quit charcoal burning and returned to our home in Nibutani after a three-year absence. My grandmother's joy was beyond description. In tears she stroked a pillar or patted her bed as she murmured, "Now I can die here in the village where I was born and raised." As though to prove her words, she left us in just two months, on January 4, 1945. Taking to her bed with a light cold, she soon passed away as if falling asleep. She was ninety-five years old according to the registration, but she was actually probably over 100.

As I said before, Grandmother was a first-rate tutor for me in my childhood. She may have enjoyed her grandson simply as good company for conversation, one to whom she could recite *uwepekere* and *kamuy yukar*. Looking back, though, I see that she securely passed down to me the great treasures of the Ainu people.

In August of the same year, in that time of destitution near the close of the Pacific war when everything was rationed, the efforts of village leaders brought electricity to Nibutani. My family was delighted when a single bare bulb was hung from the ceiling and lit up.

In February, though I was not yet twenty, I had been called up for a physical, since the military had started to move up the draft age. The examiner made a speech to exhort us: "Japan now needs new weapons. There is no weapon superior to you, bursting into enemy ranks, carrying bombshells in your hands. Are you up to the challenge of serving as the ultimate new weapon? Let me see a show of hands."

"I am!" We raised our hands simultaneously, pledging to become new weapons.

I passed the physical in the B class, becoming a member of the reserves, so I was not called up right away. That spring, however, the newspaper was filled with reports of large-scale air raids by B-29s and the defeat of Japanese forces on various islands. In late May I was drafted as a civilian in the volunteer corps. I joined Kabura Regiment 15306, led by Second Lieutenant Shimura Tarō. It was stationed at the air base at Hatchōdaira, on elevated land north of Muroran. I was employed as a worker at the base.

Barefoot or wearing straw sandals or, at best, rubber-soled toe socks with straw strings, we pushed dirt-laden trolleys on rails. Between assignments about thirty of us recruits went to the wharf at Wanishi on other jobs. On the way, we passed twenty to thirty Chinese prisoners-of-war at work. They pointed at our feet and, breaking out in smiles, chattered away with gusto. They were probably telling one another that judging from our footwear, Japan's strength must be waning. Soon afterwards, Japan was defeated.

On July 14, 1945, just one month before the war ended, Muroran was assaulted by U.S. warships and machine-gun attacks from planes flying off an aircraft carrier. That day we were in the barracks in Inoue Park in Wanishi. From 8 A.M. on, great blasts resounded under the overcast sky. We had no idea what the noises were, but a sergeant by the name of Kasamatsu told us we were being bombarded from warships.

We took cover in semi-individual hideouts called octopus holes. We had been told to use one hole per person, but since we had in fact dug holes wide enough for two people, I clambered into one of them with my friend Nitani Sōjirō, knowing that his company would be preferable to dying alone. We sat immobile in the hole, facing each other and covering ourselves with folded blankets. Boom! With a terrible noise, the dirt walls crumbled onto our laps.

Noncommissioned officers and soldiers apparently were leaving their holes now and then to watch the direction of the bullets, for we heard loud voices telling us that although we were out of the line of fire, we should not leave our holes. If I remember correctly, enemy fire from the warships lasted until noon.

The sweeping attack from the Grumann aircraft the next day occurred during work and was so sudden that we had no time to run into the octopus holes. They roared—vroom! Rat-a-tat-tat-tat-tat! My legs turning to rubber, I was unable to run. Covering my head with a garden shovel, I clung to the roots of a cypress tree.

Since my friend Sōjirō was sleeping off a cold in the barracks, I ran there after the planes had flown off. Hoisting him onto my shoulders, I hauled him to an octopus hole. Not a shot was fired by the Japanese army in response to the intermittent aircraft assaults. When I furtively peered out of our hole between shellings, I saw the Grumann aircraft attacking a Japanese cruiser, or maybe it was a destroyer. The Japanese boat counterattacked, but to no avail. The cruiser caught fire and, engulfed in smoke, disappeared from sight as we watched from Inoue Park.

Then came August 15. As usual, we were pushing trolleys. Just after midday a noncommissioned officer who had gone to hear a radio broadcast at the edge of the Hatchōdaira air base came back and, announcing the end of the workday, ordered us to return to the barracks. We milled about our quarters, wondering what was going on, until we were told to line up outside. Standing before the 200 of us civilian employees of the military, our commander, Second Lieutenant Shimura, announced that Japan had lost the war. "How much more gratifying if the emperor had told us to fight to the last soldier," he told us in tears.

My only thought then was that although Japan could not have lost, maybe, just maybe, I would be able to go home alive. It was "just maybe" because the lieutenant's words alone were not enough to convince me.

The defeat was certain, however, and from the next day we no longer pushed trolleys but began putting the camp in order. One of our orders then was to burn all diaries. Such war records could apparently be used against us should the U.S. military occupy the area.

The diaries I had kept from 1941 to August 14, 1945, were confiscated and burned before my eyes. In them I had recorded my continuous struggle as a forestry worker, surveyor, and charcoal burner, followed by my experiences in the war. This was a greater shock to me than our defeat. For one year after that, until May 5, 1946, I did not resume my journal. As I write what could be termed a record of a half life, my profound regret over the loss of those diaries intensifies.

On August 24 I returned to Nibutani with a blanket and the military uniform I had been given to wear at work. The defeat left many traces on our Ainu villages. Villagers had died in the war, some fathers never returning and the whereabouts of some husbands remaining unknown. The hardships were great for those who were left.

8

Realizing My Dream of Becoming a Foreman

IF I STAYED ON IN THE VILLAGE, I would have nothing to eat; besides, there was no sense in sitting idle there. So I decided to go out to the lumber station and worked for two months with the Kohata team of Marutake Lumber, along the Chiroro River in Chisaka, Hidaka.

In Nibutani we grew millet in our own fields as a staple, but the wartime institution of the rice ration throughout Japan introduced us to the idea of rice as a staple, and we began to depend upon it more and more. Even for someone who had money, though, rice and clothing were hard to come by.

In May 1946 Kaizawa Masayoshi, a salesman in Nibutani, invited me to join him on a trip to Hakodate to stock up on goods for his business. Since I needed to feed my young brothers, I was willing to do any kind of work and took him up on his invitation. When we arrived, we discovered we could purchase quantities of clothing with the vouchers that had been worthless in Nibutani, where there was nothing to buy. Among the many things villagers back home were sure to be delighted with were kimonos for children and open-necked shirts for adults.

My first visit to Hakodate was as Kaizawa's assistant, but from the second time on, I went as my own boss. Gathering up the ration cards in the village, I stocked up on whatever items the villagers wanted. They were pleased, and I made money, so we mutually benefited. Because of the long war, there were general shortages, so everything, not just clothing, sold well. Even straw raincoats and bamboo-weave sieves sold.

My sales route was no longer just along the Saru River but gradually expanded along the Monbetsu River. Although the parameters of my business widened, I didn't carry more supplies or make much more profit. Thanks to this job, however, I was able to trade things for rice, so my family had fewer worries about food.

As I walked my territory, I worked out a plan to build a new house. When I returned to Nibutani from charcoal making in 1944, my first thought was how wonderful it would be to have a nice house. Since I could hardly earn enough in door-to-door sales, I came up with an idea to acquire the lumber: I asked Yamamichi Matsuo, who made charcoal at Taikeshi Creek, on the east bank of the Saru River across from Nibutani, to let me help him at a rate of one-fifth of a cord of logs per workday. Busily making coal and collecting lumber in off-hours from my sales route, I was able to obtain about 2 cords of logs.

My plan was to start building in the autumn of 1947, but it snowed on November 12, and nearly 30 centimeters had accumulated by November 18, so I didn't get the logs up soon enough and had to give up the plan for that year. In the new year we started building around the time the snow melted, and the house was completed on May 8. The roof was of tiered thatch, but the house had a foundation. It was tiny—approximately 45 square meters—but incomparably superior to the one we had lived in until then.

The weather was fair that day, and about fifty villagers came out to help. To celebrate we served a 36-liter keg of unrefined home brew and about 9 liters of refined sake I had bought on ration. After the party, when the household was peacefully asleep, I stole out of bed to the brand new house and pressed my face to the pillars. It was a house with a foundation such as I had dreamed of since my underprivileged childhood.

Although it was nominally completed, I couldn't get glass windows that easily, so of the twelve I needed, I installed only the six available, covering the remaining openings with boards. I also collected the tatami mats and other furbishings bit by bit as I continued selling my wares. It took about three more years to gather everything for the house.

In order to earn enough for furniture, I also worked at the forest cultivation that had left me with such bad memories just out of primary school. My main job, there, however, was not planting trees or weeding around saplings but providing food for the foresters.

Around 9 P.M. on July 3, 1947, three food gatherers—Kaizawa Maetarō, Kaizawa Tomeichi, and I—walked past the Nioi Primary School shouldering black-market rice when a suspicious policeman accosted us. We begged him to overlook the incident, pleading that the rice was for the forestry kitchen, we three were also foresters, and without the rice we would be unable to plant trees.

The officer questioned us closely and seemed to realize we were not lying. Saying, "Well, if that's so, wait in front of the police station; I'll be there later," he went off.

The three of us reluctantly made our way to the station with the rice still on our backs and waited outside in the dark for about two hours. The policeman finally returned and "released" us, saying with a troubled expression, "The Ainu are just so honest. Don't tell anyone I found you. Now go home quickly!" On the road back we conjectured that once he had discovered the black-market rice he couldn't let it go, and ordering us to appear at the station was his way of telling us to go home. (That officer probably rose to prominence and is retired, leading a leisurely life. Even now, when I see the woods of todo pines we planted to the right and above the Baratai Creek, I recall the black-market rice incident.)

From about this time, I started working in earnest as a logger. I went out to the work site without a day of rest, and though it was not as if I were tops in production, I was third or fourth in quantity of wood cut. Because I kept away from liquor and cigarettes and worked hard, I gained the trust of my co-workers and came to the attention of the foremen. Perhaps I was desperate to become one of the foremen I had idolized in my primary school days.

Then, about 1949 or 1950, I formed a small subcontracting group and called it the Kayano team. Although I had just a few men under me, I was often chosen as representative when there were negotiations between subcontractors and foremen to improve working conditions such as workload, meals, and baths.

Having become a foreman, however small the team I headed, I decided that it seemed about time to settle down and find a bride. Since my two older brothers had died of tuberculosis, though, my family was rumored to be ridden with lung disease, my father was notorious as a heavy drinker, and there were eight people in all to live with (Father, Mother, my elder sister, myself, Sueichi, Tomeji, Miyako, and Terukazu). No matter how you looked at it, these were not favorable conditions for attracting a wife. Still, I mulled over who might be willing.

I set my sights on the younger sister of Asano, the woman who had married into the family next door. Nitani Reiko lived in the Kankan area, a recently cultivated neighborhood near Nibutani. The sixth of eight children of Nibutani's Nitani Zennosuke and Hana, she was born on tiny Okushiri Island off southern Hokkaidō on August 27, 1931. Like many other Ainu from Nibutani, her father happened to be working there at the time as a surveyor's assistant.

Her mother died of illness when Reiko was ten. From then on she was looked after by her eldest brother, Kōsuke, and his wife, and by her third sister, Asano, and her husband. She entered Nibutani Primary School in April 1938, so it seems we attended the same school for just one year.

Reiko, like me, had a large family and she lost her mother young, so her suffering was no less than mine. After the war, when there was a food shortage and reclamation projects were carried out here and there, the Kankan area near Nibutani, which belonged to Biratori village, was opened up. Reiko's oldest brother, Kōsuke, joined the reclamation project, and Reiko and her two younger brothers went with him and his wife. Their lives were one hardship after another, with nothing to eat, nothing to wear, and always doing without, but Reiko was the epitome of health, working the fields and walking the gravel roads barefoot.

Since she herself expressed willingness to join my family as my wife, I asked Kaizawa Matsuichi to act as go-between and speak to the Nitani family. Her relatives, however, would not commit and kept stalling until spring, then autumn. Conditions certainly were not favorable, as I have said, and as I had no money, having just built the house and bought furniture, I decided to save up and wait until the time was right.

We finally completed the arrangements in January 1951; I handed them an engagement gift of 10,000 yen (two payments of 5,000 yen each). Our marriage ceremony took place on March 8 the same year. I was twenty-five and Reiko was nineteen. We had the wedding at our house, inviting about fifty people to help us celebrate.

The congratulatory words of the primary school principal, Hosaka Hitoshi, fit well with my feelings at the time: "There are no complete human beings. Shigeru and Reiko are both incomplete. Please work to complement each other's shortcomings and create a wonderful home."

Our greatest luxury for the ceremony was the wedding photograph. It cost 350 yen and took me a year to pay off.

With marriage as a catalyst, I started seriously considering the idea of becoming a logging foreman. I stayed home for about five days after the wedding but then left behind my bride, Reiko, and went to work deep in the mountains along the upper stream of the

The author's wedding day.

Niikappu River with the twenty-ninth team of the Miyawaki lumberyard. I did not return for two months, until mid-May, when farming began.

I think it must have been quite difficult for Reiko until then. At home, where she had become the ninth member, she had to look after my youngest brother and care for the crops. Furthermore, I, her husband, was around only for brief intervals at the time of spring plowing and autumn harvest, otherwise working hard as a logging foreman.

In the spring of 1952, I received money from the foreman of the Matsui team, which was subcontracting for the Asahikawa National Pulp Factory, to take as many loggers as I could collect with me to Sōun Gorge in the upper stream of the Ishikari River. Matsui was from Iwachishi in Biratori, and he probably trusted me with this important matter because I was from nearby Nibutani.

Because I could not gather enough men in Nibutani alone, I asked former co-workers from Atsuga and Shizunai and succeeded in convincing over fifty loggers to go to Sōun Gorge. When we arrived, we found ourselves beyond the gorge at Mayoisawa, where even surveyors were said to have lost their way. At the time, cars could go only slightly beyond Ōbako on Sōun Gorge, and from there we had to walk. In addition, we had to carry such tools as saws and axes, our sleeping gear, and provisions such as rice. It would not have been so bad if we had needed only the usual logging tools, but we took along implements for splitting trees for pulp, so our packs were quite heavy—we were carrying about 60 kilos each. It would have been fine had we divided the load for two trips, but we couldn't bear the thought of going back and forth on the long, tortuous mountain trail, so instead we moaned and groaned as we hiked the 12 or 13 kilometers.

Making a stop midway where an ancient work station stood, we finally arrived at our destination and, putting up tents, started constructing another station. Building this was yet another strenuous task. The interior reaches of Sōun Gorge were a complete wilderness, untouched by axes, and there was such an abundance of pines ideal for pulp that sunlight barely touched the earth. There was no difficulty in clearing away enough trees to make the lodge, but the ground around the space was damp from lack of light and infested by mosquitoes and gnats, for which the location was a prime breeding ground.

It was the first time I had ever been attacked by such a huge swarm of mosquitoes. We wore starched sheer cotton on our straw hats to protect our faces, and arm covers over the cuffs of our gloves to close off our sleeve openings. Still, they managed to crawl in from somewhere, and the stings on our necks, hands, and feet itched unbearably. When we removed our gloves to scratch, the mosquitoes swarmed onto our hands, covering them until they were black. We felt stifled.

When we took off the veils to eat lunch, they would attack our faces so we couldn't enjoy the food we had so eagerly awaited. And at night the mosquitoes would come into our tents. We tried plucking grass or pulling out the cotton from our futons and setting it afire to scorch them, but the effort was wasted; it had little effect. There were several nights when we didn't sleep a wink. Once some sunlight found its way to the ground where trees had been cleared for the lodge, the mosquitoes' invasion abated somewhat. But in the beginning things were so bad that we feared we would be unable to last the workday.

Despite suffering various adversities, we finally constructed a work station that would house and feed about 100 people. The materials for the lodge were all prepared on site; specialists in various activities sawed the boards, split the chopped wood, and so on.

Among the workers were those from other small teams of five or ten. Once the nearly 100 loggers joined together at the station, a hall chief had to be chosen. The hall chief was the mediator between the laborers and the foremen. He reported the needs and complaints of workers and saw that they were properly addressed; he also passed on orders to the workers and ensured that they were carried out. The choice usually was the boss of the team with the largest number working at the lodge or someone who excelled at his job and was well liked.

On that occasion, the Kayano team, with its fifty members, far outnumbered others, so I was chosen as hall chief. When it was announced, "We propose Kayano as hall chief," and I was introduced to everyone, it took all I had to mumble in a shaking voice, "I hope to be of service." At the time I was twenty-six, rather young to do justice to the title. To be head of 100 hot-blooded, rough men was a heavy responsibility. Even so, it made me feel kind of good when older men greeted me with "Good morning, Chief" at the start of the day and "Welcome back, Chief" in the evening.

Shortly after we began the real work, one man from another team who liked to brag about his prowess as a fighter started badmouthing me. "What's with that young Ainu upstart of a hall chief?" A team member of mine who overheard the comment dragged the man outside and began to pound him mercilessly. I hate violence, so I stopped my man. This is not a pleasant topic, but the eruption of violence at the lodge was hardly infrequent.

The next morning I went with my man to Foreman Matsui and apologized. Seeing the other man with his entire face wrapped up in bandages and only his eyes peering out, I felt truly awful. After that incident, it became known throughout the camp that although the foreman of the Kayano team would not fight, he had a tough underling. People started listening to me, and I was thus able to carry out my duties as hall chief without further trouble. Kaizawa Tsunetarō gave me immeasurable help during this time.

It was absolutely draining to act as mediator in fights between loggers or deal with those who got wounded on the job, but I put my all into it, thinking it was good preparation for becoming a contractor. There actually were quite a few fights, and a number of times I found myself bundling a seriously injured worker onto a two-man rope basket for hauling dirt and carrying him over 16 kilometers of mountain trail to where a car could meet us. By surviving such experiences, I matured into a full-fledged hall chief.

9

Lucky Is the One Who Dies First

I**F** I REMEMBER CORRECTLY, it was when I returned from mountain work in the fall of 1953 that the *tukipasuy* (ceremonial wine-offering chopstick) my father had treasured above all else was not in sight. The *tukipasuy* is a revered object, believed to ensure that our supplications are heard by the gods if, prior to prayer, it is soaked in wine. That such an important utensil was missing ...

I had already noticed that whenever I came home from several months of work, one folk utensil after another used by the fireside seemed to have disappeared. And now it was the *tukipasuy* my father valued so highly.

This was eight years after Japan's defeat in the war. I had built a house and married, and it was no longer such a struggle to make ends meet. Perhaps because I was feeling more at ease, I began to see things around me I had not noticed before. Although I did not ask my father why the *tukipasuy* had gone, I resented him.

Even today I remember its shape, color, and design. It was somewhat broader than most, and the end held in the right hand was broken off, leaving only two of the three designs carved across it. If I were to see it again, I would most certainly recognize it immediately.

The tukipasuy *is used to convey gratitude to the gods.*

In those days I despised scholars of Ainu culture from the bottom of my heart. They used to visit my father for his extensive knowledge of the Ainu. I often railed at them and, accusing them of behavior as rude as that of waking a sleeping child, ordered them never to return. Professor K. of Hokkaidō University was one at whom I snarled many times. Those who sought out my father therefore learned to confirm with the neighbors that his son Shigeru was away before they came over.

There were a number of reasons I hated them. Each time they came to Nibutani, they left with folk utensils. They dug up our sacred tombs and carried away ancestral bones. Under the pretext of research, they took blood from villagers and, in order to examine how hairy we were, rolled up our sleeves, then lowered our collars to check our backs, and so on.

My mother once staggered home after I don't know how much blood had been taken. I felt that no one should go if that was how we were treated, but the village leaders rounded up people with this argument and that. And the Ainu were also compensated a certain amount.

There was also portrait photography. People not only were photographed from the front, the side, and an assortment of angles but induced to wear large number plates such as criminals wear in mug shots. Among the photographs of my mother is one in which a number plate hangs from her neck. After having her blood taken, her back checked, and being photographed while wearing this label, how much money did she receive, I wonder? My mother's pained expression in the photo always stings me to the quick.

Seeing such self-centered conduct by *shamo* scholars, I asked myself whether matters should be left as they were: Our land, Ainu Mosir, had been invaded, our language stripped, our ancestral remains robbed, the blood of living Ainu taken, and even our few remaining utensils carried away. At this rate, what would happen to the Ainu people? What would happen to Ainu culture? From that moment on, I vowed to take them back. Once I promised myself this, I believe my personality changed.

Five or six years before I came to this awareness, in my early twenties, I had tried to discard everything Ainu and even forget that I was Ainu. On February 13, 1948, a bear-sending ceremony[1] was held in Biratori with my father performing the role of the master of ceremonies. Standing aloof as my father happily dressed up and set out, I thought, "Bear-sending indeed in this modern age. Some people certainly have time on their hands!" I then headed for a nearby mountain to cut firewood, though there was no pressing need for it. Thinking back, I am terribly remorseful

---

1. A solemn ceremony in which a bear cub raised in captivity for two or three years was briefly freed and then killed to release the spirit of the god of the mountain and send him back to his world with dancing and offerings. The bear's meat was then served at a communal feast.

that I did not go to see my father's gala performance on this once-in-a-lifetime occasion.

Once I became actively conscious of my Ainu roots, I decided to start a collection of Ainu folk utensils, purchasing them myself to prevent them from being taken away for close to nothing. I first looked around our home, but there was nothing even resembling an Ainu folk piece. My father had sold conspicuous items to residents of Shiraoi—an Ainu village in southwest Hokkaidō—in the winter of 1933 or so, and nothing else could be expected to remain in our house, frequented as it was by *shamo* scholars. Still, there were my father's clothes and several wine cups, of not particularly high quality, called *isepotuki*.

The first pieces I bought in my new ambition included the *eciyus* (lacquer wine pourer) belonging to Kaizawa Maetarō. Whenever I bought a few items, the owners introduced me to others, and my Ainu collection increased slowly but surely. Since wealthy *shamo* had already purchased most objects, what remained was either particularly precious or junk—the majority being junk.

Storing the collected pieces was a challenge. Of course I was on guard against fires, but I was equally concerned with devastation by the many rats in our house. The moment I bought straw mats and the like, for example, I covered them in finely meshed wire netting.

Given the state of my finances, my buying trips never amounted to much. Still, I was determined to save money to pursue my goal and went logging in the mountains each time the season arrived. (There were two seasons: the "summer mountain" from May to October and the "winter mountain" from November to March.) Because the pay of a mountain worker was based on the amount of work he accomplished, principally woodcutting, he had to count on his own ability. Those who wished to earn money were free to work as much as they liked. As a boy, I had been apprenticed to a mountain forester and learned how to wield saws, and as an experienced charcoal burner, I was skilled at sawing. I could cut large numbers of trees without wasting energy or time.

I worked as if driven, and when I returned home to hand over money to cover the family's expenses for essentials such as rice, miso paste, and soy sauce, I rushed with the remainder of the money to houses that I had selected for their availability of folk pieces. If I succeeded in obtaining them, I was swept up in excitement. Bringing the objects home, I soaked them in lukewarm water and gently brushed off the soot, and when I found they were intact, I could not keep from smiling.

I don't think my wife, Reiko, was altogether pleased to see me carried away like this; although I provided for living expenses, I otherwise left her to her own devices to deal with life's difficulties. Even though all our remaining money was spent on folk pieces, she never once complained or looked displeased. That does not mean, however, that she was never unhappy with me, nor was I blind to her dissatisfaction.

Yet had I acknowledged my awareness of her feelings, I would have been unable to earmark money for buying folk pieces. So I pretended ignorance and continued to prepare sufficient money to buy food and warm bedding for the family, while putting aside the rest for purchases of handiwork.

People around me also wondered why I spent money on things that most others would throw out. Some even cautioned me to stop. I was convinced, however, that this apparent junk would one day be valuable and made it a rule to pay for the items so I would not later be criticized for taking advantage of former owners. Not a single item of my collection, however small, did I acquire for free. In suggesting a price, I estimated the amount of time required to make the item and its value as an antique, then tried to bid a higher price than what the seller had in mind. I have thus

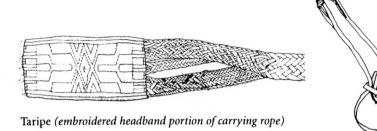

Taripe *(embroidered headband portion of carrying rope)*

never been accused of unfairness or heard complaints after a purchase.

Among the objects I pursued were two I was unable to buy simply because I didn't have enough money. One was an embroidered robe owned by a family near the Nukahira Bridge in Nioi. It was a quality Ainu robe, truly magnificent. The other belonged to the A. family in Kaminukibetsu. Of the thirty pieces they had, I had my eye on the *ecinkesapa* (sea-turtle head), divine protector of sea fishermen. I went back again and again out of my strong desire to buy it, but we were never able to agree on a price. At present, this turtle head is probably the only item missing from the Ainu folk collection at the Nibutani Museum. All the more so, I regret I did not have enough money then. (To understand why the head of a sea turtle was found in such a remote mountain area, recall Chapter 4 describing the forced exodus of the Ainu from their home near the sea.)

One day in early May 1954, when my logging work as the head of the Kayano team had begun to gain momentum (fulfilling my childhood dream), I was cultivating the field in front of my house with a horse harnessed to a plow.

A middle-aged man limped slowly past me as I followed the horse and entered my house. Thinking he might be another *shamo* scholar engaged in "Ainu study," I continued working. When I went home for lunch, I found him talking with my father, who introduced him, saying, "This is Sobu Tomio, whom I met when I went to the mainland this year." The guest seemed past forty or so. I nodded to him and ate lunch. The man ate with my father as well, but the moment I finished, I went back to work.

When I returned after dark, they were still conversing. Around midnight, the man began addressing me. His right knee apparently could not bend, so he sat with that leg stretched out and spoke with excessive friendliness: "Would you mind listening to my ideas on a certain matter, Shigeru?" He spoke glibly of wanting to take skilled Ainu performers from Nibutani to the mainland to dance at primary and secondary schools in various places and thereby "properly introduce Ainu culture. Mainlanders wrongly believe Ainu even today are solely engaged in hunting and unable to speak Japanese. This is not good for the Ainu," he finished.

At the time I resented the *shamo* for taking away Ainu folk pieces and had no interest whatsoever in "properly introducing Ainu culture." I had, moreover, come to be trusted as the boss of the Kayano team and was starting to earn a certain amount of money. I declined, saying I was uninterested in entertainment-type business.

But the man countered, "I'm not asking you to sing or dance, Shigeru. All you need do is accompany the singers and dancers and sell carved wooden bears and trays wherever we go." My father also encouraged me to go, convinced it would be profitable.

I wavered: Until then I had always lived in isolated and remote camps, moving from mountain to mountain, and I was tempted to cross the Tsugaru Strait to see the mainland. There was no way our shifty visitor could miss my hesitation. He further enumerated the many ways we could make money.

In fact, I did want the money, so I decided to do as the man said and cross the sea to the mainland. My conditions, however, were twofold. First, I would be wholly independent of the show-business side and pay for my own travel expenses. Second, I would use my own money to stock carvings and retain all profits from their sale.

I discovered later that the man had my father sign a receipt for money we never received and fill out an IOU, then quickly left the following morning.

A troupe of nine, including my father and myself, arrived at our first destination, Akita, in late May, only three weeks after the man had left Nibutani. Sobu was waiting for us as promised, having booked primary and secondary schools for us to visit. We started making the rounds of schools the following day, presenting a forty-minute program consisting of seven numbers, including dances and lullabies. Kaizawa Maetarō provided explanations and introductions. I waited out the performance without lending a hand, then conducted "business" afterwards.

In the course of listening to Maetarō's introductions for a week, however, I had completely memorized his words. One day he thrust his microphone at me, saying, "Your turn to try!" The idea of speaking in front of the audience filling the auditorium—even though they were just children—induced such anxiety that my legs wobbled. Yet the fear dissipated in a few days, and with members of the troupe flattering me with "Shigeru's better," I forgot all modesty and ended up appearing regularly on stage with everyone else.

Since a fee of 10 yen per student was charged and many schools had an enrollment of several hundred, Sobu earned several thousand yen every day. My Ainu sculptures also sold better than anticipated, and calculating that this would bring a sizable profit, I gradually became more enthusiastic about the project.

The lack of mainlanders' knowledge concerning the Ainu was exactly as Sobu had told us by our fireside in Nibutani. Even schoolteachers observed, "Your Japanese is so good" or "I see you wear the same things Japanese do." At twenty-seven, I was shocked by these comments and felt compelled to introduce the reality of Ainu people and their lives. When newspapers wrote up the impassioned way I spoke to students and teachers, microphone in hand, we started to receive invitation after invitation from other schools, and our venture seemed destined for success.

Sobu, however, had been going to drinking houses every night with the cash that came to him. Not one of us was aware of this. He never paid people on payday, but believing his promises that he would do so in a while, we continued to visit schools. Sobu, however, even started asking to borrow the money I had made from my sales of the carvings.

One night he came to see me with a woman whom we later learned a bar had sent to stick to him till he paid his debts. Claiming a calamity had struck at the home of a relative he was visiting, he asked to borrow several tens of thousands of yen. Pitying the woman who was with him, I lent Sobu all the money I had.

After touring nearly two months, we had covered Akita, Yamagata, and Fukushima prefectures, or half of northeastern Honshū. Sobu had spent a considerable amount of money and would not pay the tour members. I had borrowed 50,000 yen in order to obtain the Ainu carvings, and in addition, Sobu had wheedled me into giving him all the money either sent to our lodgings or paid on the spot from the sales. My total debt exceeded 150,000 yen.

June is a hot month on the mainland. In the midst of that heat, we were stranded without pay and robbed of our money when Sobu absconded. Having cheated us of everything, he left us behind at an inn and disappeared.

Our naivete was shocking indeed. I resented myself for having been deceived by this sleazy *shamo*. I managed to come up with money for the trip back to Hokkaidō, and we all returned to Nibutani.

But 150,000 yen was not an amount that someone who worked out of his home could quickly repay. Fortunately, we had developed a good reputation, so I formed my own tour group and led it to the mainland in September as the schools' second trimester began. I funded our trip with 50,000 yen that I borrowed mortgaging my horse and its foal.

Thanks to the practice we had gained in the spring, our seven-person show was well received. In two months I was able to repay all my debts in addition to paying the tour members. Once I had the money I needed, I left the show and hurried back to Nibutani. Having left home for months to pay off debts and pay salaries, however, I had no earnings of my own and could not look my wife straight in the eye. I stayed home only two or three days, then went off to work. I found a job deep in the mountains at the base of Mount Eniwadake, off the Chitose Railroad. During breaks I stretched out on a log and, basking in the sunlight pouring from the clear, blue sky, relished the refreshing, cool air. "After all, I'm a woodsman," I told myself.

Nonetheless, our disaster with the school tours taught me some valuable lessons. I was able to see with my own eyes various aspects of human society outside of Nibutani. My vista was also broadened by trips to scenic and historical sights as well as museums.

Around the fall of 1953, as I was collecting Ainu folk pieces, I felt I had to reevaluate Ainu culture as a whole. Gradually opening the heart I had shut tight against scholars of Ainu culture, I began to cooperate in their work.

I think it was about that time that Nitani Kunimatsu (Ainu name Nisukrekkur, born 1888), Nitani Tarō (Uparette, born 1892), and my father Kaizawa Seitarō (Arekaynu, born 1893) gathered for a conversation. They were the last three Nibutani residents who spoke fluent Ainu. As they agreed, "The first among us to die is the luckiest. The remaining two will perform *iyoitakkote* [guiding the passage to the other world] in Ainu, according to traditional ritual, so he will be certain to return to the realm of the gods. Whoever dies first is the lucky one."

"Whoever dies first is the lucky one"—I repeated it again and again in my heart. I was saddened by their words. Their import cannot possibly be grasped by those who have not been robbed of the very roots of their culture and language.

It is said that when people age, their fear of death diminishes. There is still, however, a wish to be led to the other world in an appropriate manner. The desire to die early simply for the sake of a meaningful funeral shows the extent to which culture and language are important to us Ainu.

The "luckiest" among the three turned out to be my father. Realizing that time was running short, my father sent for Nitani Kunimatsu in February 1956. Gaunt with illness, he made the following plea to Kunimatsu: "Elder brother [an appellation used as a sign of respect, even with a younger person or one without blood ties], I am seriously ill, as you can see. I cannot even dream that I will recover my strength. I would like you to perform the deathbed rite so that when I die I can return to my parents without losing my way."

Kunimatsu responded with *onkami,* the formal Ainu greeting. Then he spoke to my father slowly, in Ainu: "I accede to your request for the rite. Rest in peace, as I will recite the lines without fail. Now, although it's difficult to do this at your final moment, there is one thing I must ask you. Please answer my question fully." Our neighbors, my mother, and I held our breath in anticipation, not knowing what question Kunimatsu would pose.

"You have always been an outstanding orator. I have heard that you once threatened someone, claiming you could use your oratorical skills to place a curse of death on others. I believe it was a mere rumor, but I would like to learn, directly from you, the truth or falsity of the incident. If true, you must first apologize to the gods before I can perform the rite with a clear conscience. Also, if you threatened someone in jest without thinking, I need to intercede on your behalf. Whatever the case, I want you to answer honestly in your last hour."

We waited for my father's words, secretly fearing his answer. He answered in Ainu in a quiet, though steady, voice: "Elder brother, please don't worry. It is indeed a mere rumor. I know no such evil words as would cause others to die. In my youth, I certainly used to get carried away and pretend to know what I did not, and both my words and conduct might have misled people. But nobody taught me such evil words, nor have I ever wished to curse another to death. In the old days the lineage of one who learned such words was said to die out. I, however, have sons and their children. After I die, my children will have at least enough to eat. Elder brother, you need not worry about this. There is no need to ask the gods for forgiveness, nor do I need special intercession on my behalf."

Hearing this reply, Kunimatsu looked relieved. "I see. I'm glad I asked, though it was difficult. I am not the only witness to your reply; your wife and sons are, too. Humans with their ears aren't the only ones who heard you; all the gods in the house, especially the goddess of fire, also heard. Be at ease now." No sooner had he said this than big teardrops rolled down his cheeks, and he added in Japanese, "Seitarō, you're so lucky to be able to go first. Who will send me off when I die?" Clasping my father's slender hands in his, he could say no more. Imagining how the two old men felt, not one of us could hold back tears.

The funeral of my father, the "luckiest" because he died first, was held on February 19, 1956. As he had sworn, Kunimatsu performed a completely traditional sending-off ceremony.

I would like to explain here how the Ainu regarded curses, an issue that surfaced in the final hour of my father's life.

The act of cursing is called *iyoitakusi* in Ainu: *i* (that), *o* (to put in), *itak* (words), and *usi* (to attach). It means "to coat another with bad words." Among Ainu, eloquent people who knew many words were believed to be able to place a curse on anyone they hated. If things went smoothly when they placed the curse, all was well; but if they bungled it, the words came back to them and that disaster befell them or their families. It was also said that after their death, the members of their families would die one after another until the lineage was extinguished. I was therefore taught never to learn such curse words from anyone.

My father was so proficient in the entire range of the Ainu language that he seems to have been suspected of knowing those words. A man who fed upon flattery, he may have enjoyed the fear he elicited and maintained an ambiguous pose when the rumor spread.

Kawakami Yūji, a friend from a neighboring village, once told me, "Rumor had it that your dad knew curse words, Shigeru, but it looks like it wasn't true; you and your brothers and sisters, all six of you, are doing well. If so, a person in our village might actually have been the one who knew curses, because all his family died and his lineage ceased."

True, as my father said in his answer to Kunimatsu, the six of us live *kupoutar yayperepoka*, "not wanting for food," the condition of greatest happiness in Ainu society. I am sure he is pleased, watching us from the land of the gods.

10

The Teachings
of Chiri Mashiho

Aᴏᴛᴇʀᴇ sᴇɴᴅɪɴɢ ᴍʏ ꜰᴀᴛʜᴇʀ ᴏꜰꜰ to the land of the gods as the "luckiest" man, I continued working in the mountains during the logging season and, whenever I returned, raced around collecting Ainu folk objects.

Then, in August 1957, about a year and a half after my father's death, I met Professor Chiri Mashiho. I had heard his name long before. Around 1950 or 1951, at the invitation of Shibusawa Keizō, the three Nitani brothers—Kunimatsu, Zennosuke, and Ichi-tarō—went to the museum of ethnology at Hōya in Tokyo to demonstrate authentic methods of constructing Ainu houses. Zenno-suke, who later became my father-in-law, told me about the scholar taking notes while the brothers built the house. Chiri, I learned, was an Ainu born in Horobetsu near Muroran. Zenno-suke said he was impressed by the professor's meticulousness in taking notes—he had even asked such minute questions as whether the foothold marking the lowest layer of roof thatch should be called *iyonokicurep* (eave poker) or *aoterekeni* (stepping board). He also told Zennosuke that no matter how busy he was, he always glanced through the newspaper, earnestly explaining that one would otherwise be left behind the times.

In 1952 a Tōhoku University professor by the name of Oni Haruhito came by to hear my father speak Ainu. The professor warned us that unless more care were given to preserving the Ainu language, it might disappear from the earth. He brought up the name of Chiri as a scholar committed to the proper transmission of Ainu culture. Later, around the time that my awareness of Ainu identity was stimulated by collecting folk pieces, an October 1954 newspaper story reported that Chiri had been awarded a doctorate. I was truly impressed that an Ainu had earned a Ph.D. for research on the Ainu and, wondering what kind of person he was, hoped to meet him some day. But though less frequently than before, I was still working in the mountains, so the possibility of seeking him out was at best remote.

Then I heard that Chiri Mashiho was visiting the Biratori town hall on August 15, 1957, to record Ainu speech. Unable to resist the desire to meet him, I went to the town office uninvited. I happened to be home around that time because (as I detail later) I was making a living carving Ainu objects.

Arriving at the town office, I headed toward the conference room where the recording was to take place. Right at the entrance to the room I ran into Professor Chiri. It may sound funny to say I "ran into" someone I had never met before. But I had heard my father and my father-in-law say he was an exact image of Kaizawa Seiichi of Nibutani, so I intuitively knew that this was the famous professor. Still, I entered the room without greeting him. Having no one to introduce me, I sat in a corner of the room making myself small, the epitome of the expression *raysicupup* (as if folding oneself).

Professor Chiri soon expressed his curiosity at the presence of a man just above thirty among an otherwise elderly audience. Learning that I was Kaizawa Seitarō's son, although my surname was Kayano, the professor approached me. I have no recollection of that conversation, but I stayed until dusk to watch them record.

In the evening those who had participated in the recording session gathered to honor Professor Chiri at the home of Hiramura Kōsaku. I, too, was invited and sat near him. When the professor poured beer for me as he did for the others, I tilted my glass, whereupon he told me, "With beer, you shouldn't tilt your glass." (Ever since, whenever I happen to have a beer, I recall this occasion and make sure not to tilt my glass when someone pours for me.)

That evening Professor Chiri told me that if I had the time, I should attend a recording session scheduled four days later on August 19, at the East Shizunai home of Sasaki Tarō. I went to East Shizunai that day, was treated to dinner at the Sasakis, and stayed overnight at an inn in Shizunai.

I had no opportunity to see Professor Chiri for over a year after that, but on October 3, 1958, my wife brought me a special delivery letter from him while I was cutting firewood at a nearby mountain. The letter asked me to come to an inn at the Noboribetsu spa on the afternoon of October 4. Sitting on the chopped firewood, I read it with emotion. (Even now the letter remains one of my treasures.)

On the appointed day, I arrived at the hotel to which our meeting place had been changed and was immediately ushered into the professor's room, where he waited with a tape recorder, still a rarity then. He recorded me on various topics for two hours or so. Quite unaware of the passage of time, I talked with him and his wife, who accompanied him on that trip, over many delicious dishes at dinner. I stayed at the same hotel that night in room number 218.

About a month later, on November 7, Professor Chiri contacted me again. Wishing to shoot a documentary film on salmon fishing at the Naipetsu Creek, located between Chitose City and the Usakmay Bridge, he asked me to select people to fish and to prepare *rawomap* (fish traps) and *marep* (salmon-catching hooks).

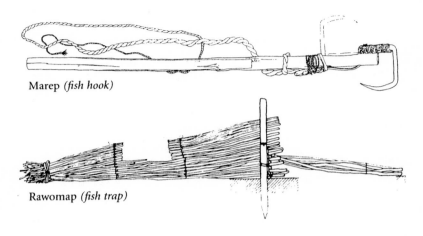

Marep *(fish hook)*

Rawomap *(fish trap)*

On that day Nitani Ichitarō, Kawakami Yasutarō, and I headed for Chitose in a truck loaded with *marep* and *rawomap*. Joining Professor Chiri at the Naipetsu Creek, we went a small distance upstream, where we checked the upper and lower reaches of the creek with nets and released between them twenty salmon from the hatchery. Giving the professor free rein to shoot while we fished by Ainu methods, we poked with *marep* or pounded with *isapakikni* (salmon-head beaters), throwing ashore the fish caught in the *rawomap*.

After the shooting, I described my childhood experiences of salmon fishing with my father. When night fell, making it difficult to distinguish whether a salmon was male or female, my father would come running and stroke its head. If he said *"Onidosi,"* I broke off a willow branch the width of a little finger and 10 centimeters in length, inserting it diagonally through the spawning mouth to the tail in order to prevent the eggs from falling. The professor repeatedly asked whether the Ainu expression for inserting a branch was *onidosi* or *onitusi*.

We stayed overnight at a Chitose inn, chatting away. The next morning, as we prepared to leave, he took my hands and said,

"Thanks to your generous efforts, I was able to get fine footage. In the future, please write down anything you hear about the Ainu, down to indelicate matters like what people of old used to wipe themselves. And record when and from whom you heard those details." It is no exaggeration to say that Professor Chiri's words motivated me to undertake my present work on a more serious level. They proved a great encouragement and guide.

Regrettably, Professor Chiri passed away three years later, at age fifty-one, on June 9, 1961. Durng his lifetime, however, he gave us Ainu a major objective and provided a role model. It is because of the appearance of a great star called Chiri Mashiho that the Ainu people came to know and reflect on themselves. The scholarly achievements he made, even as he suffered pain and agony as an Ainu, will continue to shine in our hearts as an eternal light.

From around 1957, the year I first met Professor Chiri at the Biratori town office, I started little by little to make a living by carving. It was an activity I had been engaged in for many years: In 1952, when I took fifty or so employees of the Kayano team to work in the deep mountains near Sōun Gorge, I saw a gift shop advertising Ainu handicrafts and went in to find nothing that looked genuine. From childhood, I had seen such Ainu handicrafts as Kaizawa Kikujiro's pipes and Kaizawa Uesanasi's trays, so I had grave doubts about the claim on the shop's sign. I left the shop thinking, "All right, when I get back home, I'm going to create genuine Ainu crafts."

Returning from the job in the Sōun Gorge area, I came to devote my time to carving. I went first to Kaizawa Maetarō's home and learned how to carve the fish-scale design on trays. Experimenting with the few knives in my possession, I began with a tray but then, to try something easier, worked on *tukipasuy*, practicing the fish-scale pattern.

At first, I carved only when I was home between mountain jobs, but later I also carved in the mountians when rain caused work stoppages. I gradually improved enough so that around 1954 my

In Ainu society it was important for men to be skilled at innuye *(carving). In the old days they were expected to have learned to make a mortar, pestle, and sieve before they married. The photo shows the author carving.*

pieces began to sell. By then I was able to make a variety of objects, including *tukipasuy,* trays, and *nima* (wooden containers).

From the summer of 1959 on, I made a living solely from carving. Although it did not bring in much money, I thought it far better than work in the mountains. In those days, I earned 30,000 yen in a month at the camp. Half of that amount, however, was withheld for food and other expenses. My family lived on the remaining 15,000, but this sometimes meant no money was left for me. By staying home to carve, I could make as much as 20,000. This was sufficient to feed my family and left me a small amount. I spread the word among friends I had worked with in the mountains—"It's much better to stay home and carve than go to the camps with your bedding on your back"—and so increased the number of my fellow carvers. With the tourist trade boom at its threshold, carvings were beginning to sell fairly well.

While circulating among villages to buy Ainu folk utensils with the small amount of money I saved, I saw time after time how an old man hard at work yesterday would die that morning or how an old woman was just hospitalized with illness. Although I had learned from Professor Chiri the importance of the Ainu language, I had never had the leisure to record the speech of these elders who spoke Ainu fluently. I began to realize that matters could not stand as they were: I had gathered enough Ainu folk objects to give my collection a start, and it was now time to collect the language, tales, and customs of the Ainu. This was around 1958 or 1959. I wanted to have a tape recorder for this purpose but had no money. As I was wondering how to come up with the funds, a significant event occurred.

Nitani Kunimatsu, who performed the requiem when my father died, passed away on February 3, 1960. His only remaining younger blood brother, Ichitarō, was to send him off. Thinking the funeral must be recorded, I asked permission of the bereaved family: "Kunimatsu's will be the last authentic Ainu funeral. A genuine *iyoitakkote* may never be heard after this. Kunimatsu was thoroughly familiar with Ainu customs and manners. He regretted that they were disappearing and taught Ainu scholars many things. Since he was that sort of person, I would greatly appreciate the opportunity to record his funeral." The family graciously consented.

I still had no money to buy a tape recorder, though. I rushed to the Biratori town hall, which I had rarely entered before, and asked to borrow their recorder to tape Nitani Kunimatsu's funeral. They agreed to let me use it, but since it belonged to the town council, they had me sign a loan certificate. Signing and sealing the paper addressed to "Mr. Igarashi Teiji, chairman of the Biratori town assembly," I borrowed the large tape recorder. I had an office employee set it up so it would operate if I simply inserted the cord into a socket, and I carried it home as carefully as I would a terribly fragile object.

It was February 5. Amid the weeping family members, I unwound the microphone cord to record the words of farewell with which Ichitarō, who had missed out on becoming the "lucky one," sent off Kunimatsu. Those mourners who did not know the circumstances must have thought me despicably insensitive. Cringing as I felt their unfriendly eyes boring into my back, I recorded the nearly hourlong funeral.

In September of that year, I was finally able to buy the tape recorder I so wanted. Unable to pay for it, however, I borrowed 50,000 yen from the household welfare loan fund through the Biratori town office and spent 29,000 of it on the tape recorder. As the title of the loan suggests, those funds were intended to aid families who might otherwise have had to live on welfare; that was the only type of loan they permitted at the time.

A one-hour tape then barely cost 500 yen, but getting even that amount was not a simple matter. Since I could not afford many tapes, I always transcribed the recorded materials into a notebook so I could use the tapes over again. But I found that when an old woman whose speech I had recorded died, for example, I could not bring myself to erase the precious voice and words on tape. I decided to preserve all the tapes despite the additional cost.

I now had to make more money to cover the costs of recording (tapes, transportation fees, and gifts) as well as to purchase more Ainu folk objects. Starting in 1961 I worked summers for a cable company in Noboribetsu while continuing to carve at home the rest of the time.

I was reluctant to work as an "Ainu" at a tourist site. Much of the setup violated what I had learned about the Ainu lifestyle, culture, and spirit. But the job brought in far more money than carving at home and made a substantial difference in my ability to collect and record.

I worked beside "Bear Meadow," where an Ainu-style house had been built and where we presented half-hour shows of "bear-sending" songs and dances. What in real life took place once in five or ten years was repeated there three or four times a day. It is beyond words for me to explain to others how miserable it made us feel to sing and dance—albeit for money—in front of curious tourists from throughout Japan when we weren't even happy or excited.

After the performance, tourists would crowd around and shower us with questions: "You speak Japanese well. Where did you learn it?" "What do you eat?" "Do you go to school like *Japanese* do?" "Do you pay taxes?" In the beginning, I thought that they knew the answers full well and asked those questions deliberately, just to bait us. But when those same questions were repeated day after day, I came to realize that in truth many Japanese knew nothing of the Ainu. I therefore rethought my attitude and, in addition to answering those questions with care, tried to speak with as many tourists as possible. I also did my best to explain how Ainu history, language, and customs had been vanishing (or, rather, had been made to vanish).

Despite such efforts, most visitors go home with the illusion that they have learned all about modern Ainu life from a glance at a traditionally furnished Ainu house created purely for tourists, Ainu people in costumes made to resemble authentic Ainu clothing, and the "bear-sending" made to look like an Ainu ritual. They then show their families and friends souvenir photographs while telling them about the Ainu.

This sort of thing leads to added misunderstanding of the Ainu. Many Ainu are offended by fellow Ainu who participate (or are forced to participate) in such activities at these tourist traps. But having worked as a tourist attraction, I understand the feeling of "display Ainu" so well that my heart aches. I cannot one-sidedly castigate them.

Each time I brought home the money I made as a "display Ainu," I filled my days collecting folk objects and recording Ainu speech. In the meantime, I searched my mind for ways to apply in Nibutani the experience I had gained at the resort. Hoping to improve the commercial reputation of Nibutani carvings, I invited experienced Asahikawa carvers to the Nibutani Museum, which had opened in 1962, for a workshop on wood carving. Nibutani youths who had promise to begin with improved rapidly, and, carrying their carvings on their backs, they journeyed to Sapporo and Asahikawa to sell them at gift shops.

Because of the tourist boom at that time, *attusi* (cloth woven of fiber from the *opiw* tree, of the elm family) once again came to be valued. In Nibutani the technique of *attusi* weaving had until then only quietly survived in the hands of several women, including Kaizawa Misao and Kaizawa Hagi, but with the great demand it spread in no time throughout the village.

My wife was among those who learned *attusi* weaving from Kaizawa Hagi's oldest daughter, Sumiko. It took her at least two or three years to master the technique. In *attusi* weaving she can perhaps be called a second-generation disciple of Kaizawa Hagi. In 1962, when she was finally a full-fledged weaver, she and I received a request from the humanities department of Waseda University to prepare several items for exhibit, including a patterned straw mat. The mat they had in mind was a large one, measuring 1.2 by 21 meters.

I went around asking all the old women in the village if they knew how to weave such a mat. The only one who said she knew the method added that she no longer wove because her sight was "dim," meaning lost. I decided to weave the mat with my wife.

Choosing a mat out of my collection as a model, we measured the distance between threads, then prepared a horizontal wooden bar. From this bar we hung threads wound on stones and wove as we consulted the model hung before our eyes. We were fine with the plain sections but had difficulty figuring out how to weave the patterned parts. We therefore unraveled another old mat little by little, then reproduced each step on our mat. It was not something to be learned in one sitting, however, and we wove then unraveled repeatedly until we finally mastered the technique and were able to deliver the finished mat to Waseda University. What is absorbed

The Ainu robe called attusi *is made of the inner bark of the* opiw *tree. Boiled with coal, the bark is rinsed in water then dried and torn into thin strips. These threads are twisted and rolled into balls. In the bottom left picture, Kayano Reiko stretches the thread with the help of her grandson before starting to weave.*

*This traditional cotton robe (*kaparamip*), with its embroidered patches, was worn on special occasions.*

through such painstaking efforts can never be forgotten, and from then on my wife accepted many commissions on her own.

I was engaged in these pursuits while at home, but in the summer I still worked at the tourist resort. Carving skills were also prized there, and as my work began to sell at high prices, my salary increased. But this meant that the shackles keeping me at the company grew heavier. At this rate, I thought, they would soon ask me to grow a beard to be a tourist show village chieftain. There was no denying it was a good job, in a way, as I made more money there singing and dancing than sweating at home from morning to night. I had other plans, though, and quit my job at the resort where I had worked for seven summers, from 1961 to 1967.

In 1968 I decided to open gift shops featuring Ainu carvings a short distance downhill from our house, along the national highway. Since I had no money to build stores myself, I asked Kaizawa Tadashi to build four stores that could be rented out under one roof. Kaizawa Sueichi, Kaizawa Morio, Kaizawa Mitsuo, and I opened the shops. They were the pioneers of the gift shops that stretch from Biratori to Nibutani to Nioi along Highway 237 (currently, there are fifty or so). Intimating that mine differed from other shops, I immodestly called it Kayano Handicrafts.

Sales gradually increased at the shop when the Nibutani *kotan* became a stop on the tourist circuit with the extension of the national highway through the Ikatsu Pass. Carving became my main profession. But in 1975, because it seemed everyone in Nibutani had opened a shop, I sold mine to the woman who had long managed it.

Making the Acquaintance
of Kindaichi Kyōsuke

In August 1961 I met another Ainu scholar, Kindaichi Kyōsuke, at Noboribetsu, where I was working as a "display" Ainu. Professor Kindaichi figured in one of my father's favorite anecdotes concerning researchers of the Ainu language. To the question, "What three words of great import to the Ainu have the same suffix?" Father instantly replied "*Noype* (brain), *sanpe* (heart), *parunpe* (tongue)," to which the professor smiled and retaliated, "*Siretok* (beauty), *rametok* (courage), *pawetok* (eloquence),"[1] leaving the two in laughter. Whenever my father got started talking about the Ainu language, he inevitably brought up this exchange with Professor Kindaichi.

I had had my first glimpse of the professor in the early 1960s when Professor Chiri Mashiho passed away. I had gone up to Sapporo for the wake and caught sight of him in a car by the hall where the ceremony was held. I was struck by how youthful he looked, given his great eminence.

---

1. *Siretok, rametok,* and *pawetok* were considered the characteristics of ideal men and were supposed to be requisites for those chosen as village heads.

On August 26, about a year later, the professor came to visit Hiraga Sadamo, who was working at the same tourist hot springs as I, to ask about words he didn't know in the *yukar*. I brashly asked the professor, whom I had never met, for permission to observe his scholarship at work, promising not to get in the way. "Certainly," he responded, and I was thus given the opportunity to listen intently to their exchange.

As I sat by them, listening to the professor's questions, I realized I could answer all of them. Even when Sadamo was unable to answer, however, I listened silently. The study session continued from about nine in the morning until late at night. When the day's work was almost over and they took a break, I spoke to the professor about the contents of that day's *yukar*, summarizing it smoothly. He must have been quite surprised. He peered into my face, and as he lifted and lowered his glasses, he praised me without out end, saying such things as, "So well versed at such a young age. ... The gods have introduced me to a wonderful person. I cannot but express my gratitude"—this in the presence of his assistant Murazaki, as well as Hiraga Sadamo. The professor extended his hand to shake mine as he continued, "I have never met anyone who could outline a *yukar* in such fluent Japanese. Please help me with my research in the future." This was my first meeting with Kindaichi Kyōsuke.

From then on, we exchanged numerous letters in which the professor questioned me about the *yukar*. When letters were not adequate, I went down to Tokyo and joined him at his home in Higashita-machi, Suginami. From there, we frequently went to his favorite inn, Suiyō Lodge in Atami, for a week or two of solid work.

The first time we went to Atami, the owner of Suiyō Lodge and many of her employees stood waiting to greet us as we arrived. I was startled and could only shift about nervously behind the professor. I shrank even more in embarrassment when he introduced

Kindaichi Kyōsuke (right) *and the author at the Suiyō Lodge in Atami.*

me to them, saying, "This is my teacher who has come all the way from Hokkaidō to teach me the Ainu language."

We were taken to the Sunrise Chamber in a separate building. As the first guest to stay there after the building was constructed, the professor had been asked to name it. In the raised altar was a hanging scroll with his *tanka:*[2]

> *ametsuchi no sokie no kiwami*
> > *teriwataru ōki tomoshibi taiyō agaru*
>
> **Radiating across the far reaches of heaven and earth**
> > **the sun rises, a vast candlelight.**

This was the poem he had composed on the topic of candlelight when he was invited to the poetry gala held each New Year at the

---

2. A *tanka* is a Japanese poem of thirty-one syllables.

imperial palace. It seems that on occasions when he was asked for a sample of his calligraphy, he often wrote this poem.

Dinner on that first evening was incredible. There were so many appetizing delicacies that I couldn't decide what to start with. Out of curiosity, I counted the various ingredients in the dishes and came up with approximately thirty-eight. The attendant who served our meal was named Kyōko; the professor told me he was happy whenever he saw her at the front door but at the same time saddened that she had not yet found a good match for herself.

Following breakfast at eight in the morning, we worked from about nine until five, painstakingly reading one word at a time from an old notebook into which some *yukar* had been transcribed from a recitation by Kannari Matsu.[3] I could not read the main text, as it was written in the English alphabet, but the draft Japanese translation the professor had previously recorded with the help of someone else lay nearby. If I sat too close to him, I could see the translation, and since I was afraid that this translation would affect my interpretation, I sat far away and answered his questions only to the extent of my understanding.

As a rule, whenever our day's work was done, the professor spent the time before dinner telephoning his wife in Tokyo. I remember how he asked after her health in gentle phrases and how he said, "My, how unfortunate," when he was told that Koyakko, a good friend of the poet Ishikawa Takuboku,[4] had passed away. When we lay on futons spread out side by side in the Sunrise Chamber, he would wearily tell me, as if talking to himself, "I've received an Order of Cultural Merit and in my old age I lack noth-

3. Kannari Matsu began reciting *yukar* to Kindaichi in 1927, and from 1928 on she herself recorded numerous pieces in romanized form from memory and from others' recitations.

4. The poet Ishikawa Takuboku was a slightly younger compatriot of Kindaichi Kyōsuke from Morioka Middle School in Iwate prefecture. His one-time friend Koyakko died in 1965.

ing, but because I have lived out my life, my closest friends have left me to yearn for them. My greatest regret is that there will be no friends to see me off when I die."

The professor was a very kindly person. One day the warbler he had received from the chef at Suiyō Lodge died at his home in Tokyo when he unknowingly fed it vegetables sprayed with pesticides. The professor, saddened, composed ten poems in remembrance and, writing them in brush on decorative paper, sent them to the chef.

When we tired of our lengthy sessions, we would drive from Atami over the Jukkoku Pass so he could show me the barrier ruins in Hakone or, as on my first trip, to Mount Ōmuro, where he wrote on a plain cup, ready to bake in the kiln, "With Kayano Shigeru at Mount Ōmuro Park. February 22, 1962, Kyōsuke."[5] (When I went to Atami two or three years ago, I gazed with fond remembrance on some framed calligraphy the professor had been asked to write when we made a pilgrimage to the temple of the Meichi goddess of mercy.)

On one of my early trips to Atami, I took along materials and, as he watched, carved for him my most worthy *tukipasuy*. Saying, "Since you carved this for me, let me write something for you," he went into town to buy a calligraphy card and painted, "Intentions like iron, sentiments like jewels." I take this to be a guiding principle he handed down to me, and I value it as one of my treasures.

Not every aspect of our work at Atami went well. On February 17, 1965, we faced the following situation: In one of the tales in the *yukar*, a woman betrays her fiancé. The man, angered, wraps her hair around his right hand and abuses her. No matter how we approached it, we just could not decipher *corka* in "*Wen menoko*

5. In the Edo period (1600–1868) the Hakone barrier was a major checkpoint for travelers and goods. Personalizing one's own souvenir pottery was a common tourist activity.

[evil woman], *rikun corka* [above ———], *ranke corka* [below ———], *aekikkik* [beat and beat again]."

From the details of the story, we guessed that *corka* must be something found inside the home, but the word for pillar is *ikusipe* (appearing in the *yukar* as *dondo*), a beam is *umanki*—and so we went through all the parts of an Ainu house but were unable to find anything resembling *corka*. I took it back to Nibutani as homework and upon arriving immediately asked around among the grandmothers in the neighborhood, but to no avail. Finally, Kurokawa Teshime, who lived about 8 kilometers away, solved the puzzle for me. She explained that *corka* was a condensed *yukar* form derived from *cehorka* (I'm upside down). *Rikun corka,* in other words, was *rikun cehorka* (up I go, upside down) and *ranke corka* was *ranke cehorka* (down I go, upside down). What I had considered to be the name of an object turned out to depict the motions of a person. Teshime's explanation was highly gratifying, and I sent a letter to the professor that very day.

As illustrated here, I did not know all there was to know about Ainu. Even if I had a hunch about words I did not recognize, there were times when I could not break them down to basic vocabulary. Over the lengthy period when I brought home words the professor and I could not puzzle out, this was the only example that resulted in such a clear solution.

We did not carry out our work of interpreting the *yukar* only at Atami; we sometimes worked at the professor's home in Suginami, Tokyo. This could get difficult, however, for he had one visitor after another: As he entertained one, a second would appear; once the first guest left, a third would arrive; and so on. The professor greeted every guest, no matter how busy he was. He would carry on most engagingly, and when a funny incident was related, he would remove his glasses and laugh, wiping away the tears with the back of his hand.

It was striking how many people loved him and sought him out. Sometimes I listened with them to the professor's stories, hearing, for instance, about his hardship when he was younger and had no income. Although our circumstances were different, I, too, felt deeply for him. When all the guests had finally gone, he would return to the side of the desk where we worked and drop his shoulders with a sigh. He would peer at me, saying, "After all your trouble to come down from Hokkaidō, today, too, has not been fruitful." It was on those occasions that the professor would suddenly seem an old man.

At the time, he seemed rather well off financially. Among many parcels, he also received checks from various banks for amounts of tens of thousands of yen; these he offhandedly tossed into a box. Seeing that, I thought to myself that he was being rewarded in his old age for the suffering he knew in earlier years, and that he must be content. Perhaps because he rarely spent money himself, the professor was ignorant of or, rather, unaware of financial concerns. He seemed quite out of touch with the changing monetary value of objects, so the travel expenses he gave me were based on ancient calculations or he forgot to help defray them or he paid me twice, having forgotten he had already done so once. Money aside, I went down to Tokyo time after time in the belief that Ainu and the *yukar* would thus be properly transmitted for posterity.

Still, there is one thing I rather regret. Once, when I was working with the professor at his home as usual, he started looking through the boxes nearby as if suddenly recollecting something, and he drew out an inkwell fashioned out of a clay-colored roof tile. He then told me the tile came from a famous, centuries-old building of a certain name in China and that he would give it to me. He extended it toward me, but I simply could not accept so valuable a gift out of the blue. If someone else had been there, it would have been a different matter, but thinking I could not accept when the two of us were alone, I was overly aggressive in declining it. As he looked over at me, an expression of, "Well, I guess he doesn't want it from me," flashed across the professor's face. (To this day, his face at that moment and the inkwell are irrevocably burned into my brain as one image. I sometimes wish I had accepted it, but at other times I reassure myself, "No, it's better this way. It's only because I didn't take it that I remember that inkwell even now.")

On October 6, 1968, we invited the professor to the land with which he had so long been associated, Nibutani, for an unveiling ceremony for the Kindaichi Kyōsuke Poetry Monument. About 180 people attended. With the organizer of the event, Kaizawa Tadashi, at the forefront, a highly formal ceremony was conducted in which I acted as master of ceremonies. The monument was unveiled by the professor and the two great-grandchildren of his old collaborator, Wakarpa.[6] The *tanka* inscribed on the monument was:

> *mono mo iwaji koe mo idasaji*
> *ishi wa tada zenshin o motte onore o kataru*
>
> **Saying not a word, raising not their voices,**
> **rocks merely, with their whole beings, speak their selves.**

After lunch the professor gave a commemorative lecture at the Nibutani Primary School, followed by a party at 3 P.M. He then spent the night at my home, seeming to enjoy himself. The nameplate we hang at our door today is the one he made for us on that occasion.

This trip north for the unveiling turned out to be his last to Hokkaidō. On November 14, 1971, he died, leaving behind a massive amount of literature and data on the Ainu language as a legacy for the Ainu people. His poetry monument even now stands in all its beauty as if to protect the *kotan* of Nibutani. As long as this monument remains, the people of Nibutani will not forget him.

---

6. Wakarpa, younger brother of the Shiunkotsu village chief in Hidaka county, recited *yukar* to Kindaichi in the summer of 1913.

Building the Museum
of Ainu Cultural Resources

In March 1970 I had an attack of pleurisy from overwork and was hospitalized at the city hospital in Tomakomai, about 100 kilometers from Nibutani. About eight years prior to that, in May 1962, I had contracted pleurisy from stress and, told to stay in the hospital for one month, ended up staying three. I apparently had had a relapse. But in contrast to my previous stay at the hospital, this time my mind was clouded with uncertainties. I could only fret, wondering, "If I die, what will happen to the Ainu craft items and recordings I've collected so far?" Desperate to avoid death, I strictly monitored myself to ensure recovery. As long as I had placed myself in the care of the hospital, I sternly ordered myself, I must obey the instructions of the doctors and nurses, dwell on nothing else, and completely empty my mind, not even continuing my diary.

After I made that commitment, my fever quickly decreased and I even gained weight within the first month of hospitalization, up from 60 to 70 kilos. As such, I was able to leave the hospital in mid-June. (I kept a diary from May 5, 1946; the only missing entries are from the six months or so I spent in the hospital those two times.)

Once out of the hospital, I began to think in earnest about the storage and preservation of the Ainu craft items I had collected. Over the eighteen years I had collected them, they had come to exceed 2,000 specimens of 200 types and had taken over our living room, the children's room, the hallways, the closets, and every other space imaginable. Family members seemed to be popping in and out among the handiwork in order to lead their lives, and the inconvenience to our daily activities was fast approaching the limit.

More worrisome than the inconvenience was how we would deal with fire if it broke out. The monetary aspect of the objects was of no great concern, as it came out of my own pocket, but the craftworks were the communal heritage of the Ainu, the repository of our history. I was determined, even if I had to make the effort alone, to construct a building that would serve as a museum.

First I consulted with a Biratori carpenter, Toba Ichirō. If a building without internal walls would suffice, he was willing to build one approximately 100 meters square, using discarded material, for 300,000 yen. Rather than a museum, it would resemble a warehouse. I set off to level the land near my home, then to buy the metal frames and boards for the foundation. Hearing of my plans, however, Mayor Yamada Saeichirō of Biratori, town assemblymen, and village masters came to me and explained that it would be easier to obtain money from the town if we incorporated ourselves and built a large museum for display rather than a storehouse.

I had intended to build by myself, even if I had to sell my land, and thus had received estimates from the carpenter. It would be far better for the items I had collected, though, if a large and fully equipped museum—surely superior to what I could produce with my own meager means—could be built to house them. I rethought my original plan and gave up my single-handed attempts.

The work was undertaken by the Hokkaidō Utari Association, and the Nibutani Museum of Ainu Cultural Resources Construction Project Group came into being. We were pleased to have Kaizawa Tadashi, the vice chairman of the Hokkaidō Utari Association, as president of the group, and Yamada Hidezō, an authority on Ainu place-names and president of Hokkaidō Soda, as consultant. We immediately set about raising funds, with Yamada in charge of the solicitation of larger donations, and President Kaizawa and myself responsible for smaller ones. Construction progressed smoothly, but the finances at the heart of the enterprise were hard to come by.

President Kaizawa and I dreamt of acquiring large contributions from the lumber companies that made gigantic profits by ruthlessly invading Ainu Mosir, greedily claiming ownership of our land and brazenly chopping down wholesale the trees in our mountains. That plan, however, failed miserably. The large lumber companies in Tomakomai, for example, kept us waiting for hours, then met with us only two or three minutes. Moreover, their uniform response was, "We quite understand your request and will contact you in a few days." The two of us would leave dejectedly, venting our dissatisfaction by wondering why, if that was their response, they hadn't just quickly called us in to hear our ideas.

There were many such uncooperative lumber companies in Biratori, too. Even though they had entered the mountains of Nibutani so long ago, cutting wood for charcoal as deep as the springs and completely defacing the mountains, we had to pay them five or six visits to get a contribution of 10,000 yen. Once, when we traveled all the way to Asahikawa, the woman president, who was used to giving donations, told us, "Why, how nice of you to remember us and come this way. If only you had come last year, I could have added another zero, but business is not going so well this year; this is all I can give you." She then handed us two 10,000-yen bills. Wondering if things were truly so bad, we accepted the 20,000 yen, then soon after found out that the company was commissioning a building whose cost ran into the tens of millions of yen. I suppose a 20,000-yen donation was just not the same as the millions that went into construction.

After a number of such encounters, I even complained to President Kaizawa that it would be simpler and quicker to make carvings and sell them so I could raise the funds myself rather than waste efforts soliciting. From our persistence, however, general donations exceeded 3 million yen, and we collected 2.7 million yen from Biratori, 2 million yen from the Hokkaidō legislature, and 4,350,000 from the Japan Bicycling Enthusiasts' Association for a total of 12.5 million yen.

At the time, the prefectural government set aside 3.7 billion yen for the construction of the Hokkaidō Settlement Memorial Building at Nohoro, near Sapporo. By contrast, it reluctantly provided just 2 million yen for the Museum of Ainu Cultural Resources that we Ainu were attempting to build with our own hands.

Meanwhile, a number of people we had never met or heard of sent money upon reading about our plans in newspapers or magazines. With their moral support, we set about fundraising with renewed vigor.

In the spring of 1971, about a year behind our original schedule, we started construction. By December we at last had a building, a fine museum of concrete on 150 square meters of land. The approximately 600 traditional objects of 250 types we displayed went through a rigorous selection process from among the thousands I had acquired. Nevertheless, not every possible Ainu item was available, so whatever was lacking I engaged Nibutani youths to help me create. Of course I had to pay them, and since funds had been depleted, I set off again with President Kaizawa to solicit more contributions. Securing each item, one by one, we prepared for the opening of the museum.

Finally, on June 23, 1972, we opened the Nibutani Museum of Ainu Cultural Resources to the public. The opening ceremony was held at the Nibutani Community Center, where we received exorbitant praise from the many assembled guests. I naturally was

The center of Ainu residences in the old days was the fire pit. Carving and weaving were daily activities.

happy, but I cast my eyes downward, thinking that if only these people had understood the importance of preserving Ainu culture twenty or even ten years earlier, we could have done greater justice to the transmission of that legacy. Three years before the museum opened, at the unveiling of Professor Kindaichi's poetry monument, we had vowed to make the monument the cornerstone of Ainu cultural preservation, and now, close by, there stood this museum.

The museum was the realization of my dreams, but in the midst of construction, I also had to face the sorrow of reality: On December 9, 1969, my mother died at age seventy-one. After she turned seventy, my mother had frequently repeated, as if talking to herself, "A long time ago, I was told by a respected monk"—as mentioned earlier, Mother often put up priests-in-training for the

The author's mother, 1969.

night—"that as I got older, I would experience more and more happiness. So when it's time, I'm going to die *kamuykar onne* [soundless as a withered tree falling]." I listened in silence, thinking that was surely what would happen to this woman with a heart of gold, who used to pull our bedding out from under us to offer to needy people in search of a night's lodging. Just as the monk had predicted, Mother spent an increasingly comfortable old age, free from the struggle to put food on the table, and passed away *kamuykar onne*.

Perhaps because I am something of a show-off, whenever someone I know gets married or passes away, I want to express my feelings of celebration or lament in Ainu. In fact, I recited Ainu words of mourning on the deaths of Professor Kindaichi and Professor Kubodera Itsuhiko.[1] In April 1973 Kurokawa Teshime of the old Nioi Village, Biratori, near Nibutani, died. She was the old woman who had deciphered that word in the *yukar* that Professor Kindaichi had such trouble with. She knew plenty of *yukar* and *uwepekere* and allowed me to record them on many occasions.

I was not invited to the funeral, but during breakfast the thought came to me that an expression of thanks would be appropriate. An hour before the ten o'clock services, I assembled paper and pencil, and with the drive that accompanies an act that must be completed in one try, I transcribed my Ainu words of lament in a single burst. The finished text in hand, I rushed to the ceremony, arriving barely on time. When I told the people in charge that I had prepared some Ainu words of parting for Mrs. Kurokawa and would appreciate the opportunity to speak for two or three minutes, they readily granted permission.

The funeral service was a Buddhist one, so I read my farewell to her after the sutras had been chanted and final words read. When I finished, the elders who could understand Ainu told me, as they wept tears of joy, that it had been a wonderful oration. In that mo-

---

1. Kubodera Itsuhiko (1902–1971) was Kindaichi's student at Kokugakuin University who often traveled to Hokkaidō to record *yukar*. He taught at Tokyo Gakugei University.

ment I was struck by the realization that the Ainu language lives,
that it has something that affects the core of Ainu people.

Here I present the entire text of my salutation to her:

kukor nupepo	O my holy spirit,
kukor katkematpo	O my fine lady,
unukar hetap	Do we in fact
aki katu an	see you,
tane anakne	Since by now
kamuy kar nanka	with your
kamuy kar sirka	face molded by the gods
akor wa kusu	and your body shaped by the gods
aynu itak	you perhaps feel
epuytumare	you do not wish to hear
aki rok sir	the words people speak;
koyoyra kuni p	it is not that I forget that
somo ne korka	as I speak,
kamuy kar itak	but these words
ekasi kar itak	were made by the gods
u ne a kusu	were made by our ancestors,
heru kuwanno	so I present to you
pone or kasi	over your remains
cikewehomusu	very simply put
ciekarkar na	words of comfort.
ciyaykoruska	Please
enkarkar wa	consider these
enkore yan	heartfelt.
eyasirka	Truly
itak puri ka	we could call it
aye nankora	a mosaic of words—
tane anakne	although today
tono ne manu p	those laws
kor irenka	of the Japanese people
irenka kasi	that we too
akoykar wa	have been made to learn—
akor wa pirka p	what we were allowed to own
aye wa pirka p	and what we could say
aynu itak	were
u ne rok awa	the words of the Ainu,

cikounkeske	but they were cursed
pikan koraci	and the same as others
urar sinne	like haze
rayoci sinne	like rainbows
ecancanke	the souls of words
itak ramat ka	faded
aikouk noyne	and were about to be snatched away
sir ki rapok	when at that moment,
pirka hine	as fortune would have it,
unarapepo	you, auntie—
katkematpo	O fine lady
sekor he kuye	I should call you—
aynu itak	hearing
eeraman wa	the fact
ean aan hi	that you know
kunu wa kusu	the Ainu language,
cikotetterke	I sought you out
pirka itak	and you taught me
itak humtur	not a few
eoraponko	wonderful words
ennure wa	and the best of words
kukao wa an na	that I then recorded.
tap anakne	These now
aynu itak	are Ainu words;
itak ramat ne	the souls of these words
otu sasuysir	are such
ore sasuysir	that they will be preserved
eoma kuni p	in the two eternities
ne ruwe tapan na	and the three perpetuities.[2]
kamuy mosir	Even when you have gone
sinrit kotan	to the village of our ancestors
ekoarpa	in the homeland of the gods
ne oka ta ne yakka	after that

2. The expression *otu sasuysir ore sasuysir* (two eternities, three perpetuities), repeated in the award speech, reflects a rhetorical pattern frequently found in *yukar* (as in "while dancing two dances, three dances," "shedding two pure tears, three pure tears," "our land drawn in two shapes, three shapes"). It has the effect of creating a flowing tone.

itak tuntu ne	your voice
ahawehe anakne	will continue to live
siknu wa an wa	as a pillar of our language
akor son utar	that our children
amippo utar	and grandchildren
utar tura no	will
ecanupkor pe	with their friends
ne ruwe ne na	treat as sacred scriptures.
kukor ponepo	Dear remains,
kukor katkematpo	o fine lady,
inne nispa	among these many men
katkemat utar	and their wives
utaperari	seated together,
ikir tum ta	I
nep kune wa	am
somo ne yakka	as nothing,
eramu kuye rusuy	but
tapan pe kusu	it is to proclaim
cikotetterke	your achievements
cikocinpuni	that we have come.
kuki hawe ne na	And what I say
eepaki ta	next is that
tane anakne	now
poro kur komoyo	there are few elders left
a ki wa kusu	and therefore
teeta neno	we cannot
aynu puri	as of old
somo an yakka	hold an Ainu funeral, but
ikkewe ta	lend your ears
ehekotekamuy	to the words
ye rok itak	your fire goddess speaks
ekokanu wa	first
hetat ta heta	and with speed
aoskur rok pe	find your way
ekor nispapo	to the breast
temkor kasi	of your husband
eyaytunaste	who departed before you.
hotasis kewtum	Holding on
yaykore wa	to your desire to hurry

mippo akor a	you must
sekor an yaynu	completely
somo ekor no	forget your grandchildren
eattukonno	and your feelings for them,
kamuy mosir	singlemindedly
ekoarpa kuni p	heading
ne nankor na	for the homeland of the gods.
anu ewen pe	Being spoken of
sioka yeyar	after your departure
ne akastap	in words awkward for you—
keray katkemat	as you are a fine lady,
ene akusu	this should not happen.
nep kune wa	Although I
somo ne yakka	am nobody special,
heru kuwanno	I present
pone okkasi	in simple fashion
kewe cihomsu	over your remains
ciekarkar na	words of comfort.
kukor nupepo	O holy spirit,
konkami na	I pray to you.

In 1975, for *Uwepekere shūtaisei* (The *uwepekere* anthology), in which I collected Ainu folktales, I received the twenty-third Kikuchi Kan Literature Award. Again, I gave my acceptance speech in Ainu:

Nispa utar katkemat utar sine ikir ne konkami na tapan iramuye iramuye kasi kuhekote kamuy kamuy eturen ciaskeani ram ossi wano kuyaykopuntekkor huci utar kuirwak utar kuwenmacihi kusiokote nispa maciya kamuy maciya, kukocinpun kuki ruwe ne eepaki ta tapan ikopuntek tapan iramuye tap anakne cinukar aynu kor irawe somo ne nankor aynu nomi kamuy itak kar kamuy kamuy opitta ene yaynupa hi kamuy kar itak ekasi kar itak eoraponko an rok pe rayoci sinne urar sinne ukocancanke hi kopan kusu pas utek pe ne ene iwanke wa ekasi kar itak uomarpare p ne rok kuni kuyaynu awa, sisam utar kamuy turano nukar aan hi tananto or ta tapan pe neno kuramu aye sir kupirka turen pe turen pe tura ram ossi wano kuyairayke p ne ruwe tapan na, tapan iramuye tap anakne sinen

The author and Kayano Reiko at the Kikuchi Kan award ceremony.

kune wa keunkeray pe somo ne nankor, pirka uepeker pirka isoitak ennure a unarpe utar koeturenno tane anakne kamuy nean kur huci utar ekasi utar turano keunkeray pe ne ruwe ne nankor, tapan uske ta asirkinne unarpe utar kukoonkami p ne ruwe tapan na eepaki ta sisam nispa utar kukoramkor hi ene oka hi tewano ka aynu itak aynu puri kurkasike kosneomare neun poka itak pirka p otu sasuysir ore sasuysir ooma kuni kosanniyopa wa enkore yan, sinrit itak kuye askay pe somo ne korka heru kuwanno yairayke itak cikor itak ani kuye hawe ne nispa utar katkemat utar sine ikir ne ney ta pakno nisasinu kuni kamuy punki an nankor na.

I offer a word of greeting to all who have gathered here. I am most pleased to be invited, along with the gods, to this ceremony, this banquet. I have brought with me the elderly women who narrated these tales, my brothers and friends, and also my wife. I believe that this award is in accordance not just with human ways of thinking but that the many gods the Ainu revered and the gods that created words all felt this way. Fearing that the words they created and the words our ancestors created—those that existed in no small number—would disappear like rainbows or haze, they used me as a messenger to pick up and gather together the words of our ancestors. That all of you, along with the gods, observed this and that I am so honored today delights me, as well as the gods who have possessed me, from the bottom of my heart. This prize, this object, is not something I alone am accepting. I consider this award as one

I receive along with the already departed grandmothers and grand-fathers who let me hear their fine stories, their beautiful words. Here I properly thank these old women. I wish next to implore all of you to continue to focus light on the Ainu language and Ainu culture and somehow lend your strength to ensure they will not decay in the two eternities and the three perpetuities. Although I cannot speak well the language of my ancestors, I express simple words of gratitude in Ainu. As my closing gesture, I ask the gods to look after the health of all of you gathered here.

13

As a Member
of the Ainu People

In the spring of 1975, quite to my surprise, I was nominated as a candidate for the Biratori town assembly. Since I had never had an interest in politics, I firmly declined, but those responsible for nominating me had a ready argument: "If you don't run for office, there will no longer be a single Ainu member on the Biratori town council." As a resident of Biratori who gathered Ainu craftwork and words for the preservation of Ainu culture and dreamt of a revival of the Ainu language, I could not resist pressure like that. I had no choice but to announce my candidacy. Driven around in a car especially fitted for the campaign, I went to every possible nook of Biratori, a sash with my name on it that was perhaps 30 centimeters wide draped across my right shoulder. (Biratori, I should mention, is a town the size of a small prefecture, 747 square kilometers.)

When the ballots were counted, I had received 247 votes. Supported by numerous people, I was elected to the eighth seat among twenty-two council members. Actually, I owe an apology to the people who tirelessly drove me around the large town of Biratori, for during the campaign my gaze wandered to the dilapidated horse carts, horse-drawn sleighs, logging chains, and the many worn farming tools standing in the shadows of houses I had never seen before. By the end of my campaign, I had a mental map of the locations of all the old equipment in town.

The moment I had fulfilled my postelection responsibilities, I referred to the map in my head and bought those objects. Hiring a big truck, I visited each home with a cart, a sleigh, and logging chains and asked to have them. Sometimes people even showed me the inside of their storage sheds, where I made many a serendipitous find.

If I had not run for the assembly, perhaps I would never have come across these things and they might have rotted into the earth. In the Ainu manner, I regard my chance to collect them as an act of the gods, who may manipulate a human being to perform a task they are unwilling to undertake themselves: They had this Ainu, Kayano Shigeru, purchase what they desired. Those tools are now carefully preserved, away from rain and wind, in the storage hold to the north of the Nibutani Museum. It would be wonderful one day to expand the museum to depict the evolution of farming tools from the age of the Ainu to the present day and to show the lumbering techniques of old.

Near the end of 1977, Nibutani had a visitor, Assistant Professor Ōtsuka Kazuyoshi of the National Ethnological Museum, built on the former trade fair grounds in Senri, Ōsaka. His motive in coming was to ask me to create artifacts for the Ainu display room at his museum. Up to then I had three experiences with the production of articles of Ainu daily life: in 1966 for the display room at the cable rides at the hot springs in Noboribetsu, in 1969 for the display room of the literature department at Hokkaidō University, and in 1971 for the Nibutani Museum. I was quite surprised, however, because the order from the National Ethnological Museum was the largest and most elaborate. The museum also intended to build an entire traditional Ainu house in the museum. I accepted Ōtsuka's request with pleasure.

The formal order was placed in the spring of 1978, after I submitted estimates for the entire project. I hired young men such as Kaizawa Mitsuo and Kōichi, who had an interest in woodcarving, to produce the objects and asked various women to make equipment used by women. All dedicated themselves to the tasks at which they were most adept.

We are fortunate if the opportunity to create some of the items arises just once a year. These include rice-sifting baskets made of the bark of cherry trees and other utensils fashioned out of the large trunks of tall trees. The bark for these objects, according to Ainu tradition, has to be peeled off the trees in the two or three days after June 18. If it is attempted too early, the bark will not peel from the trunk, and if it is too late, the inner and outer barks come apart and are unusable.

Spurred on by the thought that the order had come from the "national" museum of the "country of Japan," we all worked intently, using the materials and tools of old whenever possible. I thus learned how to make things I had never tried before, such as the weaving of *emusiat* (a wide sash used to hang a sword off the shoulder) and *taripe* (the broad headband comprising a portion of the rope used to carry a heavy load on one's back). Weaving these had been women's work, but there was no longer anyone who knew how to make them. We unraveled old ones in order to figure out how they were put together.

I am pleased that these crafts have been revived in our age. The Ainu dwelling in the Ethnological Museum should last half an eternity as well. I am truly grateful to the museum for this opportunity. I also believe that the accumulation in a national facility of such a collection of Ainu-related information and 300 kinds of articles used in daily life is proof that the nation has at last recognized Ainu culture. I learned from this that the role of museums is not merely to collect existing artifacts but to revive and propagate forgotten crafts.

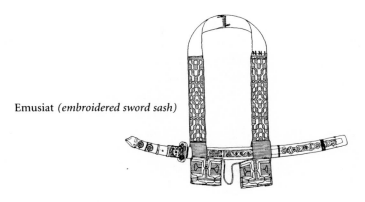

Emusiat *(embroidered sword sash)*

Of the items the museum requested, my wife made the majority of objects traditionally made by women. Since the time eighteen years ago when she labored over a straw mat woven with an Ainu design to be displayed at Waseda University, she had created all the women's articles not only for the Nibutani Museum but also for the Hokkaidō University Museum, the Otaru Museum, the Tomakomai Collection, and numerous tourist sites in the prefecture.

For me to proclaim her merits may be immodest, but once my wife starts a project, she works with great care until it is finished, never creating anything halfheartedly. I am not certain whether this determination is a characteristic she was born with or if it developed over the years as the forbearing wife who shared my poverty. Although she never mentions it, I think she must be proud of being able to create articles that will be transmitted to future generations.

In 1978 I received the Hokkaidō Cultural Promotion Award. The night I heard of the honor, I opened a bottle of beer and raised my glass to meet my wife's. I started to tell her, "Half of this award is yours—congratulations," but the rest of the words would not come. Since our marriage in 1951, my wife has withstood many hardships, not only looking after a poor family of eight

Kayano Reiko weaving.

nominally headed by a drunkard father-in-law but also tilling the fields. The husband she should have been able to depend upon left for work five days after the wedding and returned only at the busiest plowing and harvesting times in spring and autumn. On top of that, he wandered around purchasing Ainu craft items with part of the money he brought home. Our lifestyle has recently become more comfortable, but it truly used to be a daily battle with poverty.

Since I was aware of my wife's sacrifices, I tried to avoid any marital disagreements. And because as a child I hated watching my parents fight, I vowed for my three children that I would never argue with my wife. It is now close to thirty years since our wedding, but we haven't had a single fight worth recalling. I can hardly bring myself to whisper this, but it is thanks to my wife that I have been able to pursue my interests to this extent.

In February 1976 I went to China at the invitation of the Second Ainu Youth Friendship Tour. The first words I heard from the manager of the China-Japan Friendship Association who came to welcome us were, "We welcome you all not as Ainu people of the Ainu nation but as a minority nationality among the Japanese people of the nation Japan. Therefore, please do not misrepresent yourselves as members of an Ainu tribe from the land of the Ainu." I was not totally happy with his statement, but I was reassured, at least to a certain extent, as he continued, "We will not speak of nor recognize the Ainu nation, as that would be a criticism of Japanese internal affairs. The Chinese people, however, extend a full welcome to the Ainu minority nationality of Japan."

If you look up the word *people* (*minzoku*) in a standard Japanese dictionary, it says, "A social group that shares, or believes itself to share, the same racial and territorial origin, historical destiny, and cultural heritage, particularly language. Does not necessarily correspond to boundaries of race or nationality." I do not know if this definition is an official one, or if it is accepted internationally, but it is an undeniable truth that we Ainu spoke the Ainu language in Ainu Mosir and are a self-contained ethnic group.

Whenever I have the opportunity to speak to the Hokkaidō legislature, I propose the following: "The Ainu have no recollection of either selling or lending Ainu Mosir, or what the 'Japanese' have arbitrarily renamed Hokkaidō, to the 'nation of Japan.' I know that even if we were to tell you 'Japanese' to go back to the 'Japanese mainland,' it would be no easy matter for you to leave. I do not ask for such impossibilities. I wish for the Ainu and the 'Japanese' in Ainu Mosir to work together to protect our natural surroundings. I want you to put into effect policies that would effectively improve the living conditions of the original settlers, the Ainu, who have constantly suffered discrimination.

"Build homes for people who have none. Offer scholarships to serious students who cannot afford higher education. Since the Ainu are too few to be elected as Diet members or prefectural legislators, create laws and regulations that would allow us to have our own representatives. In order to revive the Ainu language and share the benefits of Ainu culture, establish, in regions that want them, nursery schools and elementary, junior high, and high schools that teach the Ainu language. Funding should be provided by the national and state governments as a form of restitution of land taxes to the yet unpaid original landholders. The country, this prefecture, and its cities, towns, and villages all lack any modicum of sensitivity regarding the issue of the Ainu as an ethnic minority. In neighboring China, regions populated by ethnic Koreans have bus schedules printed in both Korean and the standard dialect, Mandarin. In fact, all fifty-four minority nationalities in autonomous regions throughout China similarly display two languages."

In the summer of 1978, at the invitation of the mayor, I visited Point Barrow,[1] Alaska, and found that although English was the common language, in Inuit-governed parts of the city, the children were taught their native language in primary school.

I will not dwell on details, but issues concerning ethnic minorities are being rethought in earnest the world over today, and great effort is being expended to reverse the eradication of minority cultures and languages. I want Japan to take meaningful steps and not be left behind in what is happening throughout the world.

The Ainu have not intentionally forgotten their culture and their language. It is the modern Japanese state that, from the Meiji era on, usurped our land, destroyed our culture, and deprived us of our language under the euphemism of assimilation. In the space of a mere 100 years, they nearly decimated the Ainu culture and language that had taken tens of thousands of years to come into being on this earth.

Recently, there has been a move—whether initiated by national or prefectural policy, I do not know—to close down the Nibutani

---

1. An Inuit village.

Primary School and merge it with the one in Biratori. The Board of Education claims that a large school with superior facilities is bound to provide a better learning environment. Documents prepared by the board say that because children sit at desks together from a young age, there is no prejudice in Biratori. In the face of continuing and rampant discrimination against the Ainu, however, it is clear that this merger would lead to innumerable problems. There is undeniable discrimination in Biratori. Take marriage, for example. In every case brought to my attention of an Ainu and a *shamo* falling in love, the parents of the *shamo* have objected. They protest, "If the blood of the Ainu mixes with ours, we could never face our ancestral spirits again." These parents were once *shamo* children who sat side by side with Ainu students in school. Even if people state that there is no discrimination, they may still carry prejudices in their hearts. Nibutani Primary School should thus remain as it is for a while.

Much work still awaits me. The *uwepekere* I learned from my grandmother and others have been published in *Uwepekere shūtaisei* (The uwepekere anthology, 1974) but they do not account for one-fiftieth of the *uwepekere* I know. I must continue this project. The several thousand handicraft items of about 300 types I collected over a period of twenty-odd years, which I made public in the Nibutani Museum of Ainu Cultural Resources, have now been documented in the book *Ainu no mingu* (Ainu handicrafts, 1978).

Twenty full years have passed since I bought a tape recorder with money from the household welfare loan fund and started recording. Those tapes now exceed 500 hours of material. I must do something with them, for I am unable to forget the words of one old man who allowed me to record him: "Mr. Kayano, listen carefully. When you dig in the earth, you find stone and earthen implements, but not words—not the words of our ancestors. Words aren't buried in the ground. They aren't hanging from the branches of trees. They're only transmitted from one mouth to

A recent photo of the author.

the next. I beg you please to teach young Ainu their own language." I must keep working for the renewal of Ainu, the language
of a people who had no writing system.

In 1974 Professor Kindaichi's son, Professor Kindaichi Haru-
hiko, donated to our Nibutani Museum both the *yukar* I helped
the professor with at his home and at Suiyō Lodge in Atami, and
the notes of Kannari Matsu. The renewed ties inspired me to work
harder; I have decided to take up the professor's unfinished job of
translating the *yukar* into Japanese.

At this time, I spend my energy writing inadequate manuscripts, but there is so much left for me to do. If someone would
take over the task of writing, then I would build a huge nursery
school on a large piece of land and serve as headmaster. I would
speak only Ainu, never Japanese; I am certain the children would
then learn Ainu with astonishing ease. I want to quit logging, stop
carving, put my pen to rest, and become the principal of a nursery
school—that is my dream. In Ainu, dreams are called *wentarap*,

and I surely can make this *wentarap* come true. Every day I vow to myself I *will* make it real.

I, an Ainu who has been so involved with the preservation of Ainu artifacts and the revival of the Ainu language, have unexpectedly written an autobiographical work.

As far back as I can remember, I grew up in a bilingual environment where Ainu was my mother tongue and I learned Japanese as a foreign language. At some point in my youth, I became disaffected with all things Ainu. Convinced of the worth of life in the logging camps, where one's value was confirmed by strength and skill, I went as far as to become the lumber contractor of my boyhood dreams. Where and why I lost sight of this path, I do not know, but thinking that anyone could make money, I flung away the dream that had become reality and threw myself into acquiring the Ainu craftwork being taken away by the *shamo*. Now I seem to be shouldering the remains of the Ainu language and going down the road to suicide[2] with my beloved Ainu crafts.

Once in conversation with an acquaintance, I said, "If I had continued as a contractor as I'd originally planned, I might by now have been the president of a huge company," to which he gestured disagreement and replied, "Oh, no, you're no good at that kind of thing. You're too discreet; you hate borrowing money. You can be deceived by others, but you can't deceive others. You could never become a company president." Perhaps he is right.

That aside, I have let my pen scribble tales that make me blush in their fullness of shameless detail; I have written of sorrowful memories I have never before shared. I told myself, "If it's too em-

---

2. The reference is to the Japanese tradition of double suicide. When lovers were kept from being together in this world, they killed themselves in the belief that they would be united in the next life.

barrassing, I don't have to write it; if it's too sad, I should just forget it." But in the end I have recorded the truth of my upbringing and the lives of my grandparents, parents, and dead brothers. Sometimes carried away by the painful memories I was recording, I would uncharacteristically shed a few tears as my pen moved over the paper.

Wondering how readers would respond, I was torn by the thought that writing too much would make this into self-aggrandizement, whereas writing too little would not help people trying to comprehend our truth. Constantly uncertain, I have taken five years to complete this book. I published one book after another while I pushed this one further and further back. Even so, this book, written in Japanese by a man of the Ainu people, who have no writing system of their own, may be considered a monument to the Ainu.

However, because I have exposed outright the unspeakably wretched living conditions of my childhood that cannot be captured by such words as *poor* or *penniless,* I feel that perhaps I have written my disgrace rather than a record of development. If by writing this little book, which I liken to baring my body, I have made readers understand even one segment of the hardship the Ainu have been forced to bear and the road that will continue to be rough and full of grief, then nothing could make me happier.

From Nibutani in snowy February, 1980

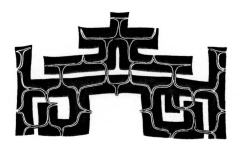

Epilogue

IT HAS ALREADY BEEN more than ten years since this book was first published, and with the publication of the paperback edition, I have been fortunate to have undreamed of numbers of people read it. That it has now been translated into English, the lingua franca, and published by Westview Press is a joy that cannot be surpassed for this untutored writer.

I would like to take this opportunity to offer readers a brief account of how my dreams and ideas unfolded and developed in the intervening years and what has become of Nibutani.

We were able to halt the proposed phasing out of Nibutani Primary School, traditionally attended by Ainu children. It was to be merged into a racially integrated school, the Biratori Board of Education promising to build a nursery school on the site of the primary school should the merger occur.

When I polled the residents of Nibutani, 125 households opposed the merger and twenty-five favored it. Those who supported the merger urged me to build the preschool. Because of my fervent desire to teach Ainu at the nursery school, I accepted the proposal and immediately established the Nibutani Preschool Construction Project Committee, of which I became chair. I contributed every yen I had to my name: 5 million. I found, however, that as villagers raised another 5 million yen, the chances increased for the continued existence of the Nibutani Primary School.

The generous donations from charitable people who heard of the nursery school that would teach Ainu added up to 5 million yen more, giving us a total of 15 million yen to bring to the Biratori township when we requested construction of the nursery school. The town accepted the money and added to it 50 million yen, including a long-term bond. The 65 million yen allowed construction of a wonderful school building; the opening ceremony was held on March 22, 1982.

We had our building, but pressure was brought to bear on us with the claim that, by national law, if preschool classes were taught in another language—that is, in Ainu rather than Japanese—the Ministry of Welfare's subsidy would be withheld.

The 5 million yen from my fellow villagers and the same amount from elsewhere, and obviously my 5 million yen, expressed a plea for Ainu instruction. I decided to try another tack: to personally fund the building of a school for teaching the Ainu tongue. Starting on October 25, 1982, I was able to realize my wish to teach children Ainu.

Observing how I built the 90-square-meter building on my own and established the Nibutani Ainu-Language School, the Hokkaidō prefectural government began providing us with 1.6 million yen annually. Biratori township assisted us with another 1.6 million, and I contributed 600,000 to meet the school's operating costs of 3.8 million yen.

With my school as the catalyst, by 1993 eleven Ainu-language schools had been established in Hokkaidō, each of them offering Ainu people an opportunity to reevaluate their own culture.

To back up a bit, when the Biratori township recognized the solidarity that constructing the preschool had fostered among Nibutani villagers, it abandoned the school merger and rebuilt our primary school. Our children have been using the new building since 1989. I take great pride in the belief that my unwavering efforts to create the preschool led to this second welcome result as well.

Concerning the Nibutani Museum of Ainu Cultural Resources that opened to the public on June 23, 1972, we were able to recreate all of the pieces for which we had names but no specimens to display: I made those objects traditionally crafted by men, and my wife, Reiko, skillfully wove and embroidered the women's things. Thus we finally had a museum that lacked not one item of Ainu folkcraft.

Seeing that space was getting tight, Biratori township indicated that it wanted to build a new museum but could not finance it so long as the articles on display were the property of an individual (namely, me). Deciding that rather than hold onto the collection forever, it would be better to preserve it in a public space, I donated all the objects on display to Biratori. For 30 million yen I also sold the township the pieces that were in storage. At market rates the collection must have been worth over 300 million yen.

Satisfied, Biratori built a separate 990-square-meter museum, transferred the entire contents of the Nibutani Museum of Ainu Cultural Resources to it, and on April 25, 1992, opened the Biratori Township Nibutani Ainu Cultural Museum. It was decided that I would run the Nibutani Museum of Ainu Cultural Resources (with some precious Ainu pieces that I had retained) as an individual, and we rededicated it on April 25, 1992, as the Kayano Shigeru Ainu Memorial Museum.

Because the existence of two museums exhibiting Ainu objects in one little village was likely to create tensions similar to those incurred when a man quarrels with the daughter he has married off, my museum began to display native crafts from throughout the world as well as from the Ainu. We put on display the objects I had bought or received as gifts on my more than twenty trips abroad, along with my personal treasures among the Ainu pieces that I kept. The collection apparently has great appeal, and we have enjoyed far larger crowds than we had hoped to attract.

I have thus spent forty years with Ainu folkcrafts and seen one museum through to completion, then started another with items from aboriginal peoples around the world to widen the horizon of my dreams. I would like to live to build this second one, too, into something worthy.

As for the Ainu language—or, rather, its words—I have completed an Ainu dictionary scheduled for publication in late 1994. It includes 13,280 words, of which 3,000 are accompanied by sample sentences. Although I received no secondary education, I believe I was qualified to compile the dictionary because Ainu is my native tongue. I wrote down every word I knew without recourse to any research materials.

For the four and a half years from October 1987 to March 1992, I broadcast an Ainu-language class, "*Irankarapte*" (Hello), every Sunday morning on STV radio.

In July 1992 I resigned as a member of the Biratori town council, on which I had served seventeen years and three months over five terms and, nominated by the Japan Socialist Party, ran for the Diet. In the multicandidate election, I fell just short of victory. I am now keeping an eye out for a vacant seat in the Diet. Having left the town council and failed to win a seat in the Diet, I am enjoying a freedom I have not known for many years.

I pray to the Ainu gods that readers of my book, as well as their families, may forever enjoy good health. Finally, I hope that you will visit Nibutani in Hokkaidō, the Ainu Mosir, serene and great land of our people.

Iyayraykere—thank you very much.

Kayano Shigeru, Curator
Kayano Shigeru Ainu Memorial Museum
September 15, 1993

Glossary

Brief biographies of persons important to the history of the Ainu people appear at the end of the Glossary (page 168).

Aca: short for *acapo*, uncle, related or not related to the speaker.
aoterekeni: stepping board, a roofing term.
asipenoka: dorsal fin.
Atsukeshi: a place in eastern Hokkaidō on Atsukeshi Bay. Matsumae Japanese drafted Nibutani Ainu to work at Atsukeshi in the late Edo period (1600–1868).
attusi: cloth woven of thread made from bast fiber of a tree called *opiw* (*ohyō* in Japanese), or garment made of such cloth.
aynu (ainu): human being.
aynu nenoan aynu: humanlike human beings.
aysirosi: arrow-end insignia.

Biratori: a town in Hidaka county.

caranke: "to let words fall," to argue.
cep: fish.
cep posunankar: small fish.
ciporosayo: rice porridge with salmon roe.

dondo: a *yukar* term for *ikusipe* (pillar).

ecinkesapa: sea-turtle head.
eciyus: lacquered wine pourer.
emusiat: embroidered sword sash.

ezo pine: a tall Hokkaidō pine that grows to 50 meters; used for home building, shipbuilding, and papermaking. *Ezo* is an old word referring to eastern Japan or to areas including Hokkaidō, Sakhalin, and the Kuriles.

hawe ruy ekasi: "strong-voiced old man," a nickname given to the author's grandfather.

hecaweni: attachment for a trap bow for catching bears.

Hidaka: one of the fourteen counties of Hokkaidō. It is west of the southern part of the Hidaka mountain range that divides Hokkaidō north to south.

hioy oy: thank you.

huci: grandma, related or not related to the speaker.

hureayusni: an ornamental branch of raspberry.

ikusipe: pillar.

inaw: ceremonial whittled twig or pole, usually of willow, with shavings still attached and decoratively curled. The size varies from 20 centimeters to more than 1.5 meters depending upon the purpose (for example, as an offering to the gods or to create a fencelike array outside a house).

isapakikni: salmon-head beater, used for catching salmon.

isepotuki: wine cup.

iyoitakkote: sending the dead off.

iyoitakusi: cursing.

iyonokicurep: eave poker, a roofing term.

kamuy: god, male or female.

kamuy ipirima: divine whisper.

kamuy oroitak: prayer to the gods.

kamuy yukar: another name for *oyna,* sacred epics of the gods, traditionally chanted by women, who were believed to personify the gods. *Yukar* are longer epics of demigods and human beings.

kamuykar onne: soundless, as a withered tree falling.

kanit: a divided stick for winding thread.

katsura: a tall, deciduous tree that grows in Japan and China, good for construction, furniture, and sculpture.

kotan: hamlet, village.

kunawnonno: Amur adonis, known as the plant of happiness and long life or New Year's plant in Japanese, belongs to the buttercup family and grows in the mountains, blooming in early spring.

makayo: butterburr.

makiri: knife, especially the double-bladed kind, measuring about 28 centimeters, used in the mountains.

marep: a type of fish hook.

marotkeciporo: salmon roe found right before the fish spawn, known as *zororiko* or *joroko* in dialectal Japanese.

Matsumae: the former Japanese province at the southern tip of the Oshima Peninsula of Hokkaidō. Mainland Japanese started to settle in southern Hokkaidō before the fourteenth century. In 1457 a warrior by the name of Takeda Nobuhiro overpowered the Ainu rebel Kosamaynu (Koshamain in Japanese). Five generations later, the Takedas were recognized as the official rulers. The family name changed to Matsumae, and their territory came to be called Matsumae province. The Matsumae became notorious for their greedy pursuit of a monopoly on fishing and the cruel treatment of Ainu.

menoko: woman, from an obsolete Japanese word; unflattering.

mosir: peaceful land; from *mo-*, a prefix meaning peaceful or small, and *sir,* meaning land, island, or mountains.

mun ewkaomap: teepee-shaped grass hut.

Nibutani: the author's home village in Biratori, Hidaka district.

Niikappu River: one of the two large rivers in central Hidaka county.

nima: wooden container.

nitope: tree sap; syrup.

noype: brain.

nupesanke: far end of a grassy field.

Okikurmikamuy: the god of the Ainu culture and principal hero in the Saru region *kamuy yukar.* Okikurmikamuy descended from heaven to the Saru region and taught the inhabitants to cultivate, weave, build, saw, fish, hunt, and worship the gods.

onkami: prayer or formal greeting with hands rubbed together then raised, palms up.

opiw: a tree (*ohyō* in Japanese) used in making cloth for the traditional Ainu robe called *attusi.*

osat: creek.

parunpe: tongue.
pattari: an onomatopoeic name for a scarecrow-like device using water.
paweto: orator.
pawetok: eloquence.
peneemo: "squashed potatoes"; potatoes left under the snow that flatten as they thaw in spring.
peraai: a special arrow used for fishing.
pewtanke: high-pitched, focused ritual call used by women in an emergency.
pipa: shellfish; seashell knife.
Pipaus: village beyond Nibutani.
Pirauturu: place-name, now Biratori.
ponkanpi: "small paper"; accounting desk.
porokanpi: "large paper"; accounting desk.
putaemo: bulbs of a wild grass in the shape of miniature potatoes.

rametok: courage.
rawomap: fish trap.
raysicupup: as if folding oneself.

sakankekam: dried venison.
sanpe: heart.
sapanpe: ornamental crown worn for ceremonies other than funerals.
sapo: big sister.
saranip: woven backsack with one strap.
"Saru Journal": An unpublished journal Matsuura Takeshirō wrote in 1858 during his stay in the Saru River basin region; "Saru nisshi" in Japanese.
Saru River: a river in western Hidaka county. The Saru River basin region produced distinguished *yukar* pieces and bards.
seypirakka: shell clogs used in games during the author's childhood.
shamo: "Japanese"; from a Japanized pronunciation of the Ainu word *sam* (side, neighbor). It is somewhat derogatory compared to *sisam*. For the Japanese equivalent of *shamo*, the author consistently uses *Wajin* (Wa people), not the more inclusive and legalistic *Nihonjin* (Japanese). *Wa* (also pronounced Yamato) is an old name for Japan.

Shiraoi: a village in southwest Hokkaidō facing the Pacific Ocean in Iburi to the west of Hidaka county, long known as an Ainu settlement and often serving as a tourist attraction.

Shizunai: a town adjacent to Biratori. The author's ancestors crossed the Hidaka mountain range westward from Tokachi and settled in Shizunai.

Shizunai River: one of the two large rivers in central Hidaka county.

sintoko: large lacquer container for food.

siretok: beauty, good looks.

sisam: one's neighbor—referring to the Japanese—from *si* (one's) and *sam* (side, neighbor).

Sōun Gorge: a gorge in central Hokkaidō in the Hidaka mountain range.

spopon: an onomatopoeic name for cut pieces of stalk of a wild plant called *putaemo.*

sune: light, special fishing method with torchlight and arrows.

tamasai: jewel necklace worn by women.

taripe: broad headband portion of a rope for carrying loads on one's back.

tasiro: large knife or dagger for use in the mountains, carried in a scabbard 50 centimeters long and 10 to 15 centimeters across. Hunters and wood cutters wore *tasiro* on the left and *makiri* on the right side.

todo pine: a variety of pine found in Hokkaidō and the the northern islands that grows to 30 meters.

topeni: sugar maple.

tukipasuy: ceremonial wine-offering chopstick decorated with ornate carvings, *Tuki* is the equivalent of the obsolete Japanese *tsuki* (wine cup), and *pasuy* is etymologically related to *hashi* (chopstick). In traditional wine drinking, the head of the family first dips the *tukipasuy* in the wine in a cup and lets the wine drip onto the fire pit while offering a prayer. He and his family take sips, then he presents the wine to the guests.

ukewehomsu: "together-chase-utter"; mutually exchanged ritual call.

uko: mutually.

ukocaranke: settling differences by argument.

umanki: beam.

uniwente: "to get angry together"; funeral for one who died unnaturally.

uwepekere: old Ainu tales in stylized prose.

wen kamuy: evil spirit.

wentarap: dream, perhaps originally *wen tarap,* bad dream. Because it was believed that talking about pleasant dreams could make the good luck they foretold disappear, it was better to call them bad dreams. If one had a bad dream, one was supposed to tell family members so they would help ward off the evil spirit. Chiri Mashiho suggests this may be the reason that *wentarap* came to mean any dream.

yasi: "scooping"; a method of fishing with a net.

yukar: Ainu epic poems, usually referring to heroic *yukar* about demigods and humans (chanted mainly by men) but sometimes including *oyna,* or *kamuy yukar,* shorter epics about the gods (chanted principally by women).

Chiri Mashiho (1909–1961): an Ainu linguist. He was encouraged to take up Ainu studies by Kindaichi Kyōsuke. Unlike Kindaichi, who worked on *yukar,* Chiri concentrated on the colloquial language. He compiled three volumes of what was to be an eleven-volume, classified Ainu-Japanese dictionary. The first botanical volume and the third on human beings were published in his lifetime, in 1953 and 1954; the second volume on zoology was published posthumously, in 1962. Chiri also left a variety of writings on the Ainu language of Hokkaidō and Sakhalin. They are included in *Chiri Mashiho chosakushū* (Works by Chiri Mashiho), Heibonsha, 1973–1976.

Kannari Matsu (1875–1961): a famous Ainu bard and aunt of the Ainu linguist Chiri Mashiho. Her Ainu name was Ikameno. She began reciting to Kindaichi Kyōsuke in 1927 and in the following year began writing down epics herself for Kyōsuke and Chiri Mashiho. She recorded numerous pieces—over ninety counting only those presented to Kindaichi—in the course of twenty-five or so years. Half of the materials in her notebooks (numbering more than seventy) are said to have been passed down from her mother, one of the greatest bards in southern Hokkaidō. Nine volumes of *yukar* from Kannari Matsu's notebooks, *Ainu jojishi: yūkarashū* (Ainu epics: collection of *yukar*), accompanied by Kindaichi Kyōsuke's annotated translations, appeared in 1957–1975 and were reprinted in 1993. The publication of the remainder of the notebooks began in 1979 under the editorship of Kayano Shigeru. Over half of the materials remain to be edited.

Kindaichi Kyōsuke (1882–1971): Linguist and pioneer scholar of the Ainu language and culture. He studied and translated *yukar* and other genres of Ainu literature and wrote on the grammar of the language. Volumes 5 through 12 of his fifteen-volume collected works (Sanseidō, 1993) relate to Ainu language, literature, and culture.

Matsuura Takeshirō (1818–1888): a Japanese official who explored Hokkaidō and the Kuriles in the late Edo. He was appointed head of the Hokkaidō Development Office under the Meiji government but quit in 1870 in protest against Japanese exploitation and plunder of the Ainu people and natural resources. Besides many journals and travelogues, he wrote *Kinsei Ezo jinbutsushi* (A record of modern Ainu individuals), which introduced some 100 Ainu from all walks of life.

Munro, Neil Gordan (1863–1942): a Scottish doctor who studied cancer in Japan. He arrived in Yokohama in 1892 and in 1898 made the first of his frequent visits to Hokkaidō. In 1923 he lost his research manuscripts, photos, and other Ainu-related materials in the Tokyo earthquake. He lived in Biratori from 1932 on. He is particularly well remembered for seeing poor patients free of charge and talking about the evils of drinking. His *Ainu Creed and Cult* was published posthumously in 1962 (London: Routledge & Kegan Paul).

Samkusaynu: the leader of the 1669 Ainu uprising in southern Hokkaidō, known as Shakushain in Japanese. In the mid-sixteenth century the Ainu on the east and west banks of the Shizunai River had prolonged fights over fishing rights. Samkusaynu, who led the easterners, persuaded both sides to rise against their real enemy, the Matsumae Japanese, and organized Ainu in other parts of southern Hokkaidō as well. They began their uprising with attacks on Matsumae trading boats. The Ainu fought successfully for two months, but the Matsumae forces, furnished with guns sent from northern provinces of the mainland, overpowered them in the end. Samkusaynu was killed when he was trapped by the enemy's pretense of holding peace talks. The Samkusaynu revolt was one of the three largest organized Ainu uprisings, along with the 1456–1457 uprising led by Kosamaynu and the 1789 uprising in the western areas on both sides of the Nemuro Strait.

Wakarpa: a famous Ainu bard born into the family that produced generations of bards, known as Wakarpa-ekasi (Wakarpa, the sire). He was a younger brother of the Shiunkotsu village head, Utomriuk. Wakarpa spent the summer of 1913 reciting *yukar* and *kamuy yukar,* also known as *oyna,* (epics of the gods) to Kindaichi Kyōsuke at Kindaichi's Tokyo home. In late August he went back to his village to pray for his sister-in-law and her family, who were ill with a contagious fever, promising to return and continue the recitation. But having contracted the fever himself, he died in early December. Kindaichi had recorded twelve *yukar* in 30,000 lines as well as *oyna* and prayers. Wakarpa had been an active hunter and gatherer, but, having lost his sight before he was fifty, his principal occupation became occasional recitation. In the fall before his death, he is said to have made fishnets and chased salmon in vain in the cold water of the Saru River, hoping to send some to the Kindaichis, who sometimes had nothing to eat but plain rice with salt or miso paste.

About the Book and Author

THIS BOOK IS A BEAUTIFUL and moving personal account of the Ainu, the native inhabitants of Hokkaidō, Japan's northern island, whose land, economy, and culture have been absorbed and destroyed in recent centuries by advancing Japanese. Based on the author's own experiences and on stories passed down from generation to generation, the book chronicles the disappearing world—and courageous rebirth—of this little-understood people.

Kayano describes with disarming simplicity and frankness the personal conflicts he faced as a result of the tensions between a traditional and a modern society and his lifelong efforts to fortify a living Ainu culture. A master storyteller, he paints a vivid picture of the ecologically sensitive Ainu lifestyle, which revolved around bear hunting, fishing, farming, and woodcutting.

Unlike the few existing ethnographies of the Ainu, this account is the first written by an insider intimately tied to his own culture yet familiar with the ways of outsiders. Speaking with a rare directness to the Ainu and universal human experience, this book will interest all readers concerned with the fate of indigenous peoples.

Kayano Shigeru is the founder and director of the Kayano Shigeru Ainu Memorial Museum. He has become a key figure in the Ainus' political and cultural revival, serving as a district representative and advocate for Ainu rights.

Kyoko Selden teaches Japanese at Cornell University. Her translations include *Japanese Women Writers: Twentieth Century Short Fiction* (with Noriko Mizuta Lippit), *Japan: The Shaping of Daimyo Culture, 1185–1868* (Yoshiaki Shimizu, ed.), and *The Atomic Bomb: Voices from Hiroshima and Nagasaki*. **Lili Selden** is a graduate student in Japanese literature at the University of Michigan.

Other Works by Kayano Shigeru

Uwepekere shūtaisei (**The *uwepekere* anthology**). Tokyo: Arudō, 1974.

Kaze no kami to Okikurumi (**The Wind God and Okikurmi**). Illustrated by Saitō Hiroyuki. Tokyo: Komine Shoten, 1975.

Ore no Nibutani (**My Nibutani**). Ainu minzoku shiriizu (Ainu people series) 1. Tokyo: Suzusawa Shoten, 1975.

Cise a kara: Ainu minka no fukugen (**Reconstructing an Ainu house**). Tokyo: Miraisha, 1976.

Honoo no uma: Ainu min'washū (**A fiery horse: An anthology of Ainu folktales**). Ainu minzoku shiriizu (Ainu people series) 3. Tokyo: Suzusawa Shoten, 1977.

Ainu no mingu (**Ainu handicrafts**). Tokyo: Suzusawa Shoten, 1978.

Yukara shiriizu (***Yukar* series**), vols. 1–13 (ed. and tr.). Hokkaidō: Hokkaidō Kyōiku Iinkai, 1979–1993.

Ainu no sato Nibutani ni ikite (**Living in Nibutani, an Ainu village**). Hokkaidō: Hokkaidō Shinbunsha, 1987.

Kamui yukara to mukashibanashi (***Kamuy yukar* and *uwepekere***). Tokyo: Shōgakkan, 1988.

Ainugo jiten (**Ainu-Japanese dictionary**). Tokyo: Sanseidō, forthcoming in Fall 1994.

IN ENGLISH:

The Romance of the Bear God: Ainu Folktales. Illustrated by Sumiko Mizushi; translated by Masami Iwasaki et al. Tokyo: Taishūkan, 1985.